Mortgage Free

How to Pay Off Your Mortgage in Under 10 Years—Without Becoming a Drug Dealer

Heidi Farrelly

ISBN: 978-0-9945171-0-4

Edited by Elaine Roughton
Cover Illustration by Sillier Than Sally
www.sillierthansally.com

Dedication

To my amazing husband.

You have supported me through all of my crazy ventures, and always believed in me.

You encouraged me when I stopped believing in myself, and together we have travelled the world, are raising a beautiful daughter, and have paid off a house!

I can't wait to retire with you and spend the rest of our lives doing what we love—together.

I love you with all my heart.

CONTENTS

INTRODUCTION

"A goal without a plan is just a wish."—Antoine de SaintExupery

Is this book for you?

- You're struggling to save a deposit and buy your first home.

- You've bought a house and are chugging along paying your minimum repayments but can't see an end in sight.

- You want to create a passive income for yourself and spend more time doing what you love, but you just can't seem to get ahead.

- You want to retire early, but it seems impossible.

If you can relate to any of the above, then you need this book!

A $500,000 mortgage takes 30 years to pay off, and over its life it will incur $579,191 in interest. That makes the total cost of your loan a whopping $1,079,191, and that's if you never redraw.

This book will show you how to pay off your mortgage in under 10 years, and knock the total cost of that loan down to $665,184, saving you more than 20 years and $414,000 dollars. This kind of knowledge is invaluable and will literally change your life, and *Mortgage Free* puts it all at your fingertips.

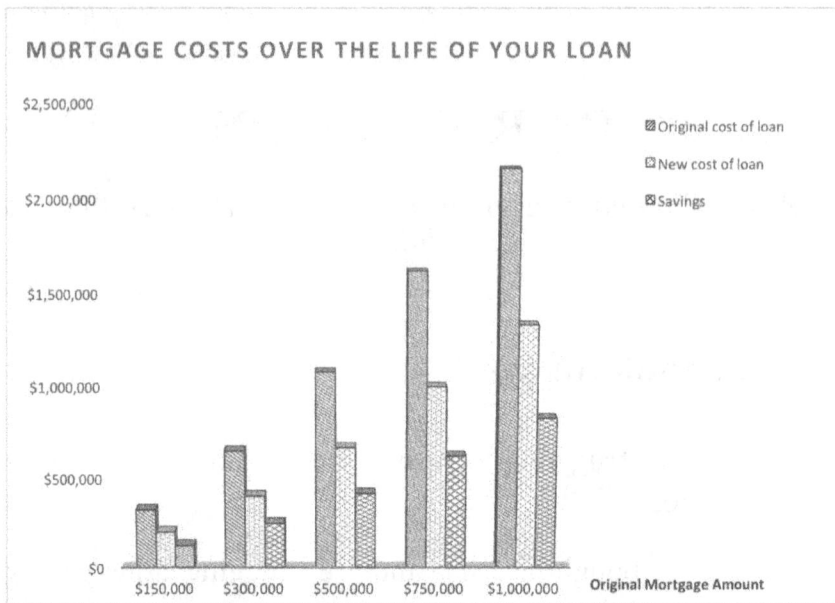

MORTGAGE COSTS OVER THE LIFE OF YOUR LOAN

Original cost of loan
New cost of loan
Savings

Original Mortgage Amount

Who I am

How do I know all this? Because I've been there, I've lived through it all, and what a roller-coaster ride it can be! We did several things we didn't plan on, like redrawing half way through our 10-year plan to pay for IVF—twice!—and we still hit our target.

We learned, we listened to advice from those around us, we did our homework and kept an eye on our figures, and it all paid off.

My family came out the other side debt free. We are happier, have more financial freedom, and appreciate the little things far more than we ever did before.

"It's not what you make, it's what you can hold onto."—
Michael Farrelly

This is something my father in-law always says. While I always agreed, I secretly thought it would be a lot easier if you made more to begin with!

Now I know the truth. It really doesn't matter what you make. You can kick and scream and cry into your coffee all you want, but the simple truth is that the more people make, the more they spend.

How extra repayments can change your life

We all do it. A $1 an-hour pay rise doesn't seem like much, and so it just gets sucked into our spending. But over the year it adds up to over $2,000! Do you know that if you took that $1 an hour and made an extra repayment of $40 a week, you would save 4 years and 10 months and $87,924 over the life of a $500,000 loan?!! For 40 bucks!! Imagine what you could do if you were really trying!

This is a fictional story, but one that is true of many families today.

Bob and Anne, and Sally and Patrick, each bought their homes for $375,000 in the same neighbourhood several years ago, and became good friends. They each had a 20% deposit, which left them with mortgages of $300,000.

Bob and Anne make $88,000 a year. They have an overseas holiday once a year, travel their own backyard every other month, and enjoy a full and active life. Oh, did I mention they also pay over half of their weekly wage into their mortgage? By doing this they will have their 30-year loan paid off in 10 years and will have only paid around $173,473 in interest.

Sally and Patrick make $142,000 a year. They too have an overseas holiday once a year, but there the similarities stop. Sally and Patrick enjoy eating out, travelling, staying in 5 star hotels, and their new house is full of nice furniture and new gadgets, and they both drive new cars. They pay the standard rate on their mortgage, and over their 30-year loan they will have paid $347,514 in interest; 20 years and $174,042 more than their friends.

Sally and Patrick might make more, but 10 years down the track they will still be continuing to pay their mortgage, while Bob and Anne will be debt free. They have set themselves up for life and can now enjoy all the things Sally and Patrick do—and so much more—without a mortgage holding them back. They just booked a 3-month holiday around the Caribbean.

This could be you!

Debt free ain't easy

If you thought there was no way you were ever going to be debt free before you reached retirement, think again. It's not easy, but it is definitely doable! By the time you have finished this book you will have been shown how to budget, how to cut your excess spending, how to save a deposit while paying debt or raising a family, what and where to buy, and ultimately how to pay off your mortgage in under 10 years instead of 30.

Becoming debt free is not all roses and sunshine, but I promise you if you follow even *some* of the solutions in this book, you will be free of your mortgage years ahead of your peers. You don't have to give up everything you love doing, either; in fact, I have dedicated a whole chapter to continuing the things you love. Life is for living, and I plan on living it!

This book will change your life. Want to know how some people own 5 homes while you're struggling to pay off one? Do you want to know how to be mortgage free at 40? Do you want to work less and spend more? I promise these are not pipe dreams! I started where you are now, and I wish this book had been around when we first bought.

It is possible. It is achievable. Sometimes you've just got to be pointed in the right direction. This book is applicable to everyone, everywhere, and will show you how to make the most out of your mortgage, your property, and your future. Just remember, *"It always seems impossible until it is done."— Nelson Mandela*

The longer you wait, the harder it becomes to get ahead. *Mortgage Free* shows you how to change simple things, straight away, that make a massive difference to your loan term. If you want to put your mortgage behind you and start living the life you've always wanted, then read on, and take back your future.

Because being debt free is the ultimate gift you can give to yourself, and your family.

CHAPTER 1
SUSTAINABLE BUDGETING

"Do not save what is left after spending, spend what is left after saving."—Warren Buffet

Budgeting—a dirty word

Nobody likes to hear the word 'budget.' It's up there with 'diet' in the dirty word stakes, but the reality is, if you don't know what you spend your money on you just can't save.

There are many different ways to go about budgeting. Just Google 'writing a budget' and you'll get hit with a multitude of options.

Unfortunately, they all assume you know what you're spending your money on every day.

It might seem like a no-brainer. Of course you know what you're spending your money on—you're the one spending it!

It doesn't always work that way, though, especially in today's world of direct debits, credit cards and interest-free finance.

We have calculators on our phones, apps that can tell us how many calories we've eaten, watches that can record our sleep, and credit cards we don't even need pin numbers to use.

The world is full of timesaving devices, but they all still need some form of input from you, and budgeting is no different.

Budgeting is seen by many as something that only old people do.

And you'd be right.

But look at those same 'old people' and you'll see they are in a much better financial state than most of us.

You are the only person who knows what you spend money on, your indulgences, your ongoing expenses, and the things that are important to you. There is no single budget that is the same as another. When you write a budget, there is no point writing something you would like to have, you have to make one that is sustainable, not just for a few months but for the life of your loan.

The importance of budgeting

Creating a great budget is the single most important thing you can do BEFORE buying your property. Your budget will tell you:

- How much you have left at the end of every week

- Any areas you can cut your spending in

- How much you can afford to spend on a house

- What and where you can afford to buy now, and if there are any rate rises

If you've already bought your property, it can help you achieve a savings goal sooner and give you more of an idea when it comes to re-mortgaging or investing.

There are a million budget spreadsheets on the Internet and the thing they all do in common is the very thing that is guaranteed to make them fail.

You write in how much you earn, followed by what you spend on big things such as rent, utilities, bills, food, etc., and you are left with whatever's left over. Pretty simple, right?

And if you are a monk, living in the middle of nowhere, who has no friends to buy presents for, no weddings to attend, no Christmas' to splurge on, and no pubs to crawl, then you'd probably be sweet! But if you are a little bit more normal than our friend the monk—it just ain't gonna work!

The elephant in the room here is that all those big bills you've written in, they only make up a portion of your life, and as such, you are only getting a snapshot of your spending. No matter how bad, you have to know what you're spending before you'll know what you can save.

How to budget

1. **Write a budget the way you would like it to look.**

   You know those Internet spreadsheets that don't work? Yeah, grab one of those and fill it out.

   Include how much you would like to spend on each item, keeping how much you earn in mind and make sure to include how much you would like to save. Now put it away out of sight for a month. Not in one of those safe places where you'll never find again—you need it later.

2. **Find something to record on.**

   This could be a notebook and pen, the 'notes' function on your phone, a draft email you can open from phone, iPad, or computer, a Word doc—whatever, just make sure it is always accessible.

3. **Write down EVERYTHING you spend.**

   I don't just mean the bills and the present you bought your mum. I mean the change you put in the parking meter, the school excursion you paid for in gold coins, the round at the pub, the coffee on the way to work, and the other coffee you *'didn't'* buy on your lunch break. EVERYTHING.

   Don't forget to include your quarterly and yearly bills like car insurance, power and water bills, property rates, health insurance, etc., and the 6 debt baddies below.

   - Student loans (include interest payments).

   - Personal loans (include interest payments).

   - Credit cards (include estimated interest payments).

   - Interest-free finance (when do you start paying interest again and how much will they be?).

   - Ongoing memberships—include everything from gyms and lessons to Netflix and Spotify.

   - Direct debits—this includes phone bills, school fees, insurances, and power.

   All these things need to be included in your budget.

   I know it seems like a lot, but believe me, when you're hinging the next 10 years of your life on it, you want it to be right!

4. **Do this for 4 weeks.**

   Is this a massive pain in the butt? Yes. Of course it is. Why would I pretend otherwise? But this is also the best groundwork you can do before buying a property. If you can't even stick to writing down a budget for 4 weeks, there is no way in hell you're gonna make it through 10 years of fast-tracking your mortgage, so dry your eyes and get writing.

5. **Collate your data.**

   At the end of 4 weeks, sit down and collate all your data. Make yourself a spreadsheet or print ours[1] and sort all your spending into groups.

   - Eating out—including lunches/coffees/alcohol
   - Going out—including movies/holidays/clubbing/aquarium
   - Bills—power/water/rates
   - Regular payments—car/phones/swimming lessons/health insurance
   - Petrol and other travel expenses
   - Groceries
   - Odds and ends—parking/donations/school and work bits
   - Retail therapy—clothes/electronics/shoes/music/DVDs

---

1 http://www.how2without.com/bonus-materials/mortgage-free-workbook/

6. **Get your totals.**

   This is the scary part. Finding out how much you actually spend on things you don't really need and never knew you wanted...

   Subtract this from what you earn and what you have left is your free money. If you have anything left. A lot of people find that although they are earning good money and not spending what they think is a lot, by the time they add in all the incidentals and day to-day expenses they are running at a loss.

7. **Find that monk budget you put in a safe place.**

   Remember that crappy spreadsheet budget you wrote, the perfect one that would never work? Grab it out and compare it to your real life one. Go over all the differences and write them down as shown in the example.

   Your reality is usually going to be somewhere in the middle of each of the two figures. Sometimes you'll find they line up, if you're lucky, and other times there is just no way the two will ever be friends. Check out the graph below. It is a perfect example of how cutting back in some areas can give you a lot more money where it counts—without cramping your style!

REAL - MONK - TRUE - BUDGET COMPARISON

	REAL BUDGET	MONK BUDGET	TRUE BUDGET
Mortgage/Rent	$400	$400	$400
Groceries	$180	$100	$150
Petrol	$120	$70	$100
Bills	$250	$150	$200
Spending	$150	$50	$50
Savings	$0	$330	$200
TOTAL	$1,100	$1,100	$1,100

8. **Trim.**

This is the hardest part of budgeting and the part people suck at the most. Sit down with your partner or your imaginary friend and really look at your spending. See where you can make cuts (the next Chapter, *Cutting the Fat,*' deals exclusively with this), save money, and dial back.

9. **Stick at it!**

Okay, so maybe this is the hardest part of budgeting. Sometimes the changes you make just don't work, and other times they are a lot easier than you imagined. A lot of it is trial and error; the important thing is to have a goal and stick to it. If you spent more in one area this week, it has to come from somewhere, and it can't be your mortgage account, so another area has to suffer.

10. **Nothing is forever.**

> Everything changes over time. Children are born, cars break down, jobs are lost and gained, and life interferes in a million different ways. Your budget therefore changes too. HOWEVER... how much you put into your mortgage can *never* change if you want to get it paid off in under 10 years. This means that when you originally write your budget, you have to be absolutely certain you are putting away an amount that is sustainable in the long term, no matter what crops up.

Reviewing your budget

Over time you may find a bit of non-essential spending creeping back into your carefully worked budget.

Don't be afraid to take another look at it whenever needed and see what might have changed.

Bills normally increase every year, and supposedly so do our wages, although this can be a bit of a joke. You will probably need to re-write your budget occasionally, but be sure you are still making your extra payments and leaving yourself enough to live on.

Key Points:

- A good budget is vital to your success, but most don't take into account those everyday expenses that really add up.

- Make certain you include ALL your expenses when budgeting.

- Review your budget periodically, always ensuring your mortgage payments remain the same, or increase.

Hopefully you now know how to write a great budget. Learn how to cut back in the next Chapter, *Cutting the Fat*, so you can stick to it, and don't be afraid to revise it every so often if you need to.

CHAPTER 2
CUTTING THE FAT

"Beware of little expenses, a small leak will sink a great ship."—Benjamin Franklin

Now that you've written your budget, you can see all the places where you can trim the fat. Or maybe you can't. We are notorious for only seeing those things that we don't mind changing and skimming over those things we refuse to let go. So let me make it simple for you.

Unless you need something to survive, to hold onto your job, or to keep your health, it can be cut. And no—that doesn't mean your $380 hairdressing bill can stay, or the $1,000 on new tools, or that gym membership. I mean bread and butter, appropriate work clothing (not new every season), and medications you actually can't live without. Everything else can go under the axe. I'm talking about the smokes, your coffee addiction, your cronut fetish, and the pokies. Whatever the thing is that makes you bleed money every month, cut it!

There are always alternatives. If you find you can't cut something out completely, just limit it so you can only spend a set amount each month. Normally have 2 coffees a day? Try cutting it to 1 and go from there. Love the cinemas? Rent the DVD instead, and pay a fraction of the amount. Hit the pavement instead of the gym; it costs you nothing and you still keep fit. I get my hair done at a friend's who runs a hairdressing business from home. Not only does it only cost me $35, but it is also the best haircut I have ever had!

How to save money around the home

- Buy a slow cooker. Yes, you're spending money, but you can pick up a new one for 40 bucks and you will save much more than that in the long run. They are considerably cheaper to run than an oven. If you live somewhere without an oven, then you can cook a multitude of things at home instead of eating out, and they make even the cheapest cuts of meat not just edible but truly delicious. There are a million recipes online for every type of slow-cooked meal. Just Google and go.

- Cook your meals at home and freeze the leftovers for future use. Always cook more than you need so you can save some for those nights you just don't have time to cook. Make sure you portion up your meal before eating, though, so you don't go back for seconds or thirds!

- Yes, cooking at home seems to take a bit longer than getting fast food, but if you prepare ahead, and know what you're having and have your ingredients on hand, you'll find that it's often quicker. I find that deciding what to have takes the longest time, and if you take advantage of the hundreds of meal planning apps and print-offs, you should be sweet.

- Draft-proof your home. While windows and doors only take up 5-10% of a home's surface space, they can account for as much as 30% of its heat loss! You would be surprised how much you can save by buying some cheap rugs and curtains from IKEA or Walmart and using them to keep drafts out from around windows and through floors. Buy a weather-sealing strip for under the door, or make yourself a draft snake. All these things will keep your house warmer in the cold weather, meaning you turn on the heater less.

- When you do turn on the heater, set it a couple of degrees lower than normal and put on a jumper. It is not only better for our power bill, but has been proven to be better for our bodies to be cooler in winter and warmer in summer. You can also watch TV with a blanket over you instead of turning on the heater. We did this for a whole winter once just to see if we could, and while there were a few nights I almost caved, we did manage it. Of course, we live in Sydney, where the lowest temps are about 4° Celsius (39° Fahrenheit) overnight. We do keep our daughter's heater on low throughout winter, however, as she tends to get coughs and colds more often if we don't. Just use common sense to judge whether you need a heater on or just another clothing layer.

- Use a lot of water? We pay for our water in Australia, and even if you don't, it is one of our most precious resources, so it's always good to try and save it where you can. Try using a timer in the shower to limit your water use (long, hot showers are my kryptonite). Wash your clothes on the economy setting and a cold wash to save both power and water. You may have to do some trials to see what works best for you. I found that I could do a short warm wash or a long cold wash, but couldn't do a short cold wash as the clothes just didn't come out as clean. You can also put a bucket in your shower to collect water for your garden, or set up a grey water system to make use of all your wastewater.

- Use fans instead of air-conditioning. We may not get cold winters in Sydney, but we get some cracking hot summers, with temperatures frequently in the high 30's or even low 40's (98°-110° Fahrenheit). We don't use air-con very often—only on the hottest days.

Instead, we put ceiling fans in every room. Even running them all night we only use a fraction of what we would if we were running air-con. You can also beat the heat by going for a swim in a lake, river, or beach, having an icy drink, or a cold shower.

- Dry your clothes on the line or on airing racks instead of in the drier. People living in apartments, small spaces, or very cold, wet areas will find this harder than others, but even in these circumstances, if you keep on top of it, a rack will hold a whole load of clothes and will dry in a couple of days. You will save a bucket load of electricity doing this, not to mention they just smell better with sunshine and fresh air.

- Don't leave electronics on standby, or do what I'm doing now and run a laptop and a computer at the same time! It might be easier to leave things on standby, but they suck a surprising amount of juice even when they're 'asleep.' If you use your laptop at work or at cafés, see if you can charge them while you're there, to save on power use at home!

- If you are a chronic tea drinker like my husband, consider investing in a stovetop kettle. Jugs are one of the highest electricity pullers in the whole house, and when you're turning it on multiple times a day, it really adds up. Another saver is to only turn the jug on when you actually have time for a cuppa. How many times have you boiled the jug 5 times before actually making yourself a drink? Only putting in enough water for your needs is another option, as it takes less time to boil a small amount.

- Buy home brand. Often the supermarket brand product will come from the same factory as the dearer ones and just have plainer packaging. Go to the supermarket with a list so you don't buy things you don't need, or overbuy and end up wasting food. Buy in-season produce, as it is usually cheaper and fresher. Don't be afraid to shop around.

- If you have special dietary requirements, check 'normal' foods' ingredients. You'll often find you can eat many of them, without paying the overblown prices for 'gluten free,' 'dairy free.' You can also bake your own a lot cheaper than buying allergy specific foods, by substituting acceptable ingredients for those you cannot use.

- Check catalogues and specials and take advantage of them. Our dog eats a lot, and whenever his brand of dog food is on sale, we go and buy a whole trolley full. Do the checkout girls think we're crazy? Probably, but as I save a couple hundred dollars, I really don't care. Mostly.

- Shop in the evenings when a lot of fresh baking and meats get discounted, and then use or freeze as desired. And I probably don't need to tell you this, but never shop hungry! Your trolley will end up full of all sorts of random items you never would have bought normally!

- Grow your own veggies. If you have a decent backyard, this can be a huge money saver, especially if you focus on the things that are always quite expensive. Even if you live in an apartment, it is achievable. Salad bowls, hanging pots of herbs, strawberries, and growing walls all take up minimal space and provide fresh, free produce. Some storebought veggies can even be re-grown from the scraps, such as potatoes and spring onions.

- Preserve, bottle, and dehydrate food while it is in season so you can eat it cheaply all year round. These things are easier to do than ever before, and don't take much practice or money to set up. My favourites are stewed pears and dehydrated mango and banana.

Streeetching your dollars

- Buy in bulk. Stores like Costco make buying in bulk cheaper and easier than ever before. You can also buy boxes of fruits and veggies at farmers' markets and wholesale distributors. Be aware, though, that buying in bulk has its drawbacks. While it offers much cheaper prices, those savings are lost if food is wasted or you eat twice as much of it because it was 'cheap'.

- The best way to avoid these problems is to share with a friend (or two). Buy a box and split it between you, with each paying a portion, OR, only buy bulk for long-life things such as cans of food or cleaning products. And if you do buy fresh, use the abundance to preserve, freeze, or dehydrate it for later.

- Buy cheaper cuts of meats and alter your recipes to suit slow cookers, casseroles, and soups. You can also soften cheaper meats by marinating them or smashing the crap out of them with one of those little meat hammers. Extend your repertoire and include vegetarian meals in your weekly menu. They are delicious and generally cost less than meat-based ones, although personally, my family prefers meat with their vegetarian...

- Swap meals with a friend. If you get bored of making the same things or it's easier to make 3 big meals than 6 smaller ones, grab a friend or 3 and organise a meal swap. While it might not be any cheaper, it will give your palate some new things to try without eating out, which will save you money. Basically, you cook a giant meal, separate it into however many people are participating, and give one to each. They do the same, meaning you all have meals for the week and have saved time cooking.

- Learn to do things yourself. Whether it's changing your oil and water, hanging curtains or blinds, or building a kitchen, you can find tutorials on You-Tube or ask a friend or family member to share their knowledge. We bought an IKEA kitchen when it was time to replace ours. I put all the cabinetry together myself, and my husband and father-in-law installed it and fitted the bench top. We saved over $10,000 by not hiring someone else. Not only is this achievable, it is very rewarding. And did I mention you'll save a bucket load?

- New season, new clothes, right? Don't get caught up in fashion craziness. If you're old enough to be buying a house, you should have figured out what suits you by now. Make your wardrobe a statement of you rather than of others. Wear what you find you are comfortable in and be confident.

- Each season, buy one or two things that you need or want, but make sure it complements what you already own so you don't have to buy a whole new wardrobe.

When you can afford to, buy quality over quantity, and it will last. I have jackets and boots that I have worn for 15 years, and while I may have re-soled them or had them dry-cleaned, they still look fabulous and get a lot of use. Even though they cost more to begin with, they have worked out considerably cheaper in the long run.

- If you absolutely must have a huge wardrobe, then you'll need to consider where and how you shop. Check out thrift stores, eBay, department store sales, and factory outlets. Buy plain tops and bottoms that can be dressed up to look more expensive than they actually are.

- Lunch money. Gone are the days where everyone took their packed lunch to work. Cafés do a roaring trade around business areas, as people use their lunch times to queue, order, and pay for exorbitantly-priced sandwiches, wraps, and meals-to-go. There is, though,

    a slow shift back towards packed lunches as people begin to realise the health, cost, and time benefits of bringing their own.

- I know, I know... you don't spend much on lunch, But in reality, unless you're getting your whole lunch for $3-$5, it is cheaper to BYO. Okay, let's check the figures. You spend $10 a day getting a drink and a chicken wrap for lunch (some people spend a lot more than this!). Packing the same lunch from home, down to the chicken and drink, would only cost you $4. So, 5 days a week, 48 weeks a year (hopefully you're not at work 52), you have spent an extra $1,440 on lunches alone.

- This does not include coffee, breakfast bagels, or afternoon ice creams. If you took that $30 a week and added it to a $500,000 mortgage instead, you would save a whopping 3 years and 2 months and $72,307 dollars. How's that for a free lunch!

- As you can see, the smaller the mortgage the bigger impact these changes make. The larger the mortgage, the more changes you will need to implement.

BASED ON PACKED LUNCH SAVINGS OF $30 PER WEEK

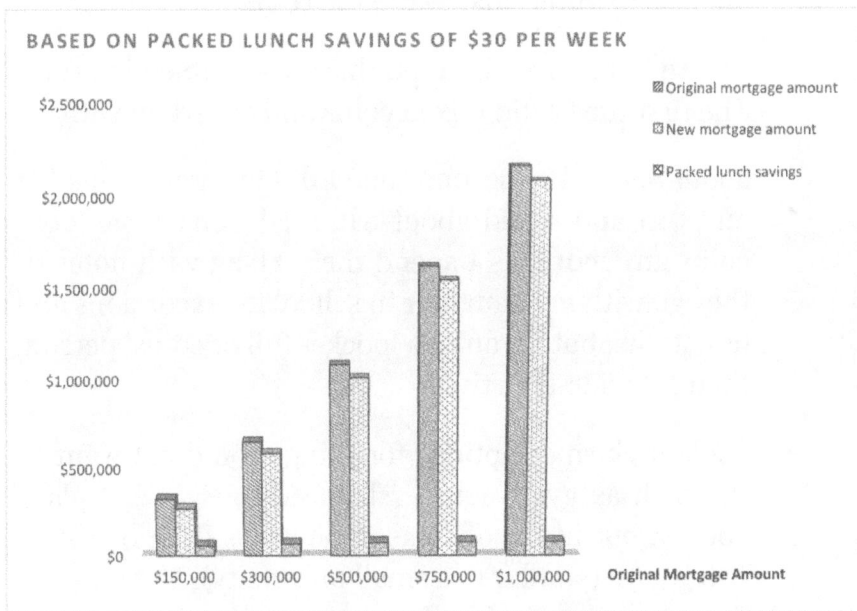

Legend:
- Original mortgage amount
- New mortgage amount
- Packed lunch savings

Y-axis: $2,500,000; $2,000,000; $1,500,000; $1,000,000; $500,000; $0

X-axis (Original Mortgage Amount): $150,000; $300,000; $500,000; $750,000; $1,000,000

- How much are you paying in insurance, power, and gas? Do you even know? A lot of people don't. If you're like me and have had health insurance for over 10 years, then you just pay it each month and sigh every time they put the price up. Researching big bills like health and pet insurance, power, and gas can not only ensure you're not getting ripped off, but can help you get some great deals and discounts. Shop around and don't be afraid to ask companies if they offer discounts for long-standing members, direct deposit, or a lock-in contract.

- Save your coins. A lot of people carry pockets full of loose coins that eventually get lost, spent on coffee and ice creams or thrown in the corner of a drawer. Buy yourself a money tin that can't be opened until you use a can opener on it, and start putting your coins in. Not only will they add up, but you won't find yourself buying frivolities just to use the coins.

- Before I had my child I did this for a couple of years. The first time I did mixed coins and ended up with

  about $400. The second time I did just gold coins ($1 and $2) and saved about $1200! I don't have loose coins any more, as I spend them along with notes or they go with my daughter to school for excursions and donations, but if you're a 'pocket full of coins' person, then get yourself a tin.

- Look at cheaper options for things you don't want to cut such as gym memberships. My neighbour plays hockey, but in the off-season he keeps fit at our local Tafe's gym (similar to a small university). Not only are the rates considerably cheaper than a privately-owned facility, he has also been able to participate in 10-week personal training sessions several times when students are ready to be assessed. For free! Can't get much better than that!

- Got a coffee craving? You and half the population! Coffee is one of those things people see as a necessity, and that's fine. But even with coffee there are ways to lessen the blow. Make your own before you leave home and take it in a travel cup. Limit the amount of coffees you buy in a day. Normally buy 3? Aim for 2 next month, and maybe even 1 the month after.

- Take sachets to work with you so you can make your own instead of purchasing, or take advantage of free coffee at your workplace. If you have to buy coffee, shop around. Some places offer special deals, discounts for local businesses, coffee cards that get you a free one after a certain amount paid for, and one shop I walk past near work offers a 50 cent 'karma discount' for bringing your own coffee cup. Awesome! For 2 coffees a day, 48 weeks a year, you would save $240, or $12,533 over the life of a $500,000 loan. Now that's some good karma!

Phone bills: This is just one of many bills that you can look at in an effort to cut back. Use this example to assess other things in your budget from every angle.

Phone bills—one of those things that start off relatively small and can grow out of all proportion. First, you need to look at how much you use your phone, what you use it for, and how much you pay each month.

- Do you need a landline? Many people often just have mobiles now, and if you don't call overseas or need the Internet connection, you could scrap it altogether. Work out if it is cheaper to pay more on your mobile bill or to pay for both.

- Going over your cap? You will often find that if you are going over your cap each month, paying more for a higher cap will actually work out cheaper.

- Kids keep running up bills on your phone? Put a lock on it and don't let them use it. We never had them growing up. They see their friends every day at school and there is a plethora of things to do in the world besides social media. Adults usually need to take that under advisement too.

- If social media is an issue, turn off all the notifications and set yourself times when you can check your social media. Not only will this save on bills, but it will free up your time, too. A *lot* of your time!

- Take advantage of free Wi-Fi when you're out and about and save your data for when you have no access to the free stuff.

- Go prepaid. If you are still struggling to keep within your budget, switch to prepaid and don't recharge more than your set limit each month. Emergency calls can still be made without credit, so don't use that as an excuse.

- Paying for kids' phones too? Don't! If they are old enough to have a phone they are old enough to pay for it as well. This might not be in the strictest sense of paying, but put a limit (prepaid is easiest) on their spending and get them to do jobs, etc., to earn it.

- Utilise the apps. Skype, WhatsApp, Facebook Messenger, and many more are making messaging and face-time, not to mention photo sharing, even easier, at a fraction of the cost of using your phone's network. Check them out and work out which works better for you. Don't forget to add data use into your calculations.

Grabbing a bargain

I love getting a bargain, who doesn't? Sometimes, however, bargain hunting can make us spend money we didn't really need to. If you stalk your local buy/sell/exchange and get all their updates on your mobile or email, stop! I had to remove our local sellers' app from my phone because things I 'needed' kept popping up! There is no easier way to spend money than by rationalising it to yourself. Saving 70% is great, but if you didn't need it in the first place, you just spent 30% more than you needed to.

"A bargain ain't a bargain unless it's something you need."—Sidney Carroll

A friend once said something I found hilarious, and which really puts it into perspective. "My wife bought a packet of crackers with 75% less fat, but then she ate the whole box! Why doesn't she just buy the crackers she likes and eat ¼ of them?"

This is the same with bargain hunting! If you're specifically looking for something, then by all means, get out there and grab a bargain, but if you're snagging a bargain just because it's 'cheap,' then you're doing yourself a disservice. Save that money and use it to buy things you actually want and need.

Cars

They are fabulous. They save time, they make life logistically easier, and they are clean and dry. Sort of. (Never drive in my car...) But do we really need to use them as much as we do? Sometimes I think we just get so used to jumping in the car we forget some places are close enough to walk. So what I want you to do is really think about when you actually need to use the car.

Can you take public transport to work? By doing this, you could potentially be saving money on fuel, maintenance, and parking. Can you walk with your kids to school or to the shops? Can you bike? Can you car pool with a friend or work colleague? Can you share a car with your partner instead of having 2?

There are two companies in Sydney that are revolutionising the way we see cars. One is Go Get[2]. This company has car 'pods' in strategic places around the city where you can pick up a car when needed, and you pay for only the time you use it. When you're finished you return it to one of the car pods. It doesn't have to be the same one. People who usually use public transport and don't own a car use Go Get when they are picking up groceries, taking a day or weekend trip, or visiting somewhere like IKEA. It works out much cheaper for them to do this than to own a car and pay all the related costs.

The other company is Car Next Door[3]. This company is quite new but has been going incredibly well, as it has filled a niche market. Car Next Door combines car owners who like the convenience of having a car but don't use them often and those who don't own a car but use one occasionally. Essentially, you can rent your neighbour's car. It's really cool.

Key points:

- A bargain is not a bargain if it is something you don't need.

- See things differently. Just because you've always done things one way, doesn't mean you can't change.

---

2 www.goget.com.au
3 www.carnextdoor.com.au

- Don't cut things out completely; find an alternative or use as many tips as possible to minimise your spending.

There are many other ways to cut the fat, from making your own cleaning products to creating your own gifts. Find out what works best for you, to get you as close to your desired budget as possible, and then tackle the next Chapter, *Make More—Save More*, where we look at how to earn, and keep, more money in your pocket.

CHAPTER 3
MAKE MORE—SAVE MORE

"Don't be too busy earning a living to make any money."—
Joe Karbo

How to make extra cash and save a deposit

How do you save a deposit when you're paying off debt? Or paying your way through college? Or supporting a family on one wage?

This is hard. Not "Oh I had to do 20 push-ups at the gym today" hard—I mean really hard.

Why? Because when you're in debt, paying rent, have no deposit, and are earning a mediocre wage, it really does feel like you have no way to get ahead.

If you read *Chapter 2: Cutting the Fat*, you should already have some ideas about how you can trim the excesses in your life. If you had no excess to trim in the first place, then here are a handful of tips that may help you out.

You may be resistant to some of the more profitable ones such as house sharing, but when you have very few options, you need to make the most of the ones you do have.

- Rent out your garage or your driveway for some extra cash, especially in the inner city, where car spaces are hard to come by and you can pay up to $50 a day for parking. This can be quite lucrative, and renting your driveway or garage is not even very invasive to your life.

- Renting your spare room on the other hand, can be invasive. It can work really well, however, if you know the person, you can get exchange students, or if they have a few references. I would always recommend vetting them in some way first, and I personally wouldn't do it with young kids in the house, although I know people who do this and have no problems. Look for people who have trusted professions such as teachers, nurses, and airline staff, all of whom need security clearances of one kind or another in their chosen fields. Make sure you protect yourself with insurance and a lease.

- Price up the cost of a granny flat. Do you have a garage that could be converted to a granny flat or a large block where one could be placed? Do your sums and work out if this would be worth it for you, or if the cost of the flat would outweigh the income.

Our neighbours have a granny flat at the rear of their property and they have a long-term renter who is absolutely lovely. She can access her flat down the driveway, so it is not an invasion of personal space for either her or the family, and they get about $250 a week.

That's an extra $13,000 a year, less expenses like water and power, which would be minimal. Added to a $300,000 mortgage, this could save you almost 18 years and $223,112 over the life of your loan. And you've increased the value of your property!

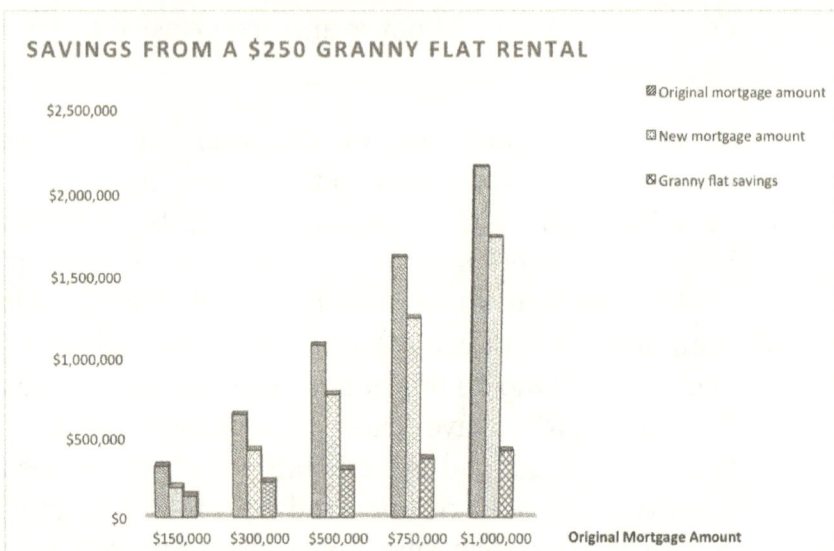

SAVINGS FROM A $250 GRANNY FLAT RENTAL

Legend:
- Original mortgage amount
- New mortgage amount
- Granny flat savings

Y-axis: $0, $500,000, $1,000,000, $1,500,000, $2,000,000, $2,500,000

X-axis (Original Mortgage Amount): $150,000, $300,000, $500,000, $750,000, $1,000,000

- Have fruit trees or a veggie garden? Could you? Fresh fruit and veggies sell really well, and if you don't use sprays or pesticides, they are naturally organic (although not certified). Once the word gets out you have fresh lettuces, lemons, and herbs, people will come a-knockin'.

- I saw a magazine article not long ago about a couple who made quite a bit of extra cash growing and selling plants. Things like daisies, lavender, and succulents don't even need seeds. You can just break a piece off, stick it in soil, and watch it grow. Bromeliads and other 'clumping' plants you grow until they are large enough to separate, and then you have 2 or more individual plants. While you wouldn't get thousands of dollars, you could certainly make hundreds, especially with the flaxes, bromeliads and other, more expensive plants. Sell them on eBay, local pages, at your front gate, or at markets.

- Do you love to cook? Set up a meals or baked goods page on Facebook or Wordpress[4]. You could offer specific things for people to order, or you can offer single people, busy families, or the 'cooking challenged' home-cooked meals. This could be as simple as making twice what you normally would each night: 1 to eat and 1 to sell. You could also do bespoke food planning and recipes for people, providing them with specific meals and snacks that work with their food allergies, time constraints, and diets.

- Look at companies such as Kitchen Surfing[5] for ideas. They only operate in New York at the moment, but their business model is super cool. Don't forget to check food safety requirements with your local council. In some places, selling anything cooked in your kitchen without certification is illegal, so make sure you do your homework first.

- Do you like dogs, or at least don't hate them? Put out some flyers, or pin signs to your local noticeboards, and offer yourself for dog walking or pet sitting services. You'll find that people (especially in the inner city where yards are small or non-existent) are relying on services such as this more often now.

- House sitting. There are websites you can add your name to worldwide to offer yourself for house sitting. Not only do they pay you, and sometimes pay you very well, but also your living expenses other than food are free for the duration of your stay, saving you more at home.

---

4 www.wordpress.com
5 www.kitchensurfing.com

- Freelance with the skills you have in any free time you can carve out. This might be writing content for someone's website or blog, doing graphic design, developing websites or apps, taking photographs for companies such as Shutterstock[6] and I-stock Photo[7] or babysitting in your local area.

- Make and sell craft, jewellery, or anything else you're good at on Etsy[8] or at local markets.

- Write and sell e-books. If you think you have knowledge or a story that people would be willing to pay for, then go for it. Did you know that over 80% of the population wants to write a book but only 1% actually do it? If you need some help getting started, check out Self-Publishing School[9] and QuitN6[10] for some great ideas and FREE info.

- Teach or tutor. If you've ever taught or excelled at a subject, then pass on your knowledge to others. You can pick the hours to suit you, and either do it face to face or set up an online course on sites like Udemy[11].

- Staff special events and conventions. This could be things like attracting attention for a store, handing out merchandise, or dressing up as a mascot.

- Become a mystery shopper and make that trip to the store pay for itself by getting paid for assignments by market research companies.

---

[6] www.shutterstock.com
[7] www.istockphoto.com
[8] www.etsy.com
[9] https://xe172.isrefer.com/go/curcust/HeidiF (affiliate link)
[10] http://www.quitn6.ontraport.com/t?orid=8475&opid=1 (affiliate link)
[11] www.udemy.com

- Request a raise! It doesn't cost you time or money, and the worst that can happen is a bit of hurt pride and a no answer. Often a company likes that you have been gutsy enough to ask, and even if they don't give you a raise, you may find yourself watched for advancement more closely.

- Get paid to run errands for others or shuttle people around in your car.

- Clean homes, mow lawns, rake leaves, or shovel snow. You can do these on an ad hoc basis or on a permanent basis and get around $10-$30 an hour.

- Sell your unwanted gold, your hair, your clothes. Have a yard sale. Minimise.

- Collect bottles and cans or recycle scrap metal for cash.

Looking outside the box

- Think outside the square and get your celebrants' license—they can earn between $300-$600 per wedding for an hour's work.

- Got a car? Cover the expenses by using it as a mobile billboard. You know those cars you see covered in advertisements? I always thought they were company cars, but it turns out you can get paid from $400$1000 per month, depending on the length of the campaign, to advertise on your car. Some companies will even provide the car! Check out Free Car Media[12] and AdverCar[13].

---

[12] http://freecarmedia.com/
[13] http://advercar.com/

- Rent your car out with companies such as Car Next Door.

- Transcription. Often people record sound files and videos and then need them transcribed. If you have a good grasp of the written language and can type, this could be for you.

- Set up a Bed and Breakfast. While this is not for everyone, it may work well for people who live in the countryside and can't take advantage of some of the other options. Set up a free website on Wordpress, advertise on Airbnb[14] and other local sites, and take some nice photos. Photos really sell a place for me. Make sure you list local attractions and sights and be friendly! You will need at least 1 room with an ensuite or a separate cabin/flat.

- Use your body—not like that! Sign up for focus groups, which pay between $10 and $500 for your opinion on products, participate in medical research studies for anywhere between $50 to $5000 depending on time and invasiveness, or become a standardised patient (basically acting sick for medical students) for around 20 bucks an hour.

- Sell your eggs, sperm, extra breast milk, or plasma. You can make up to $60 a day selling breast milk, $20-$125 per sperm donation, and $20-$45 per session selling plasma (you won't get any money for blood donations, just that wonderful feeling that you've helped others). Selling your eggs could net you up to $5000, although this is both an exhausting and invasive undertaking. Really think about how you feel

---

[14] www.airbnb.com

about any of these things and how they may affect you and your family long term.

- Chickens! Some councils don't allow you to keep chickens in your backyard, but a lot do, and you can have quite a few chooks in an average yard, either free ranging or in a hutch. Fresh, free-range eggs are always in high demand, and you can get around $4-8 dollars a dozen for them. Do your research on the different types of hens and which would be right for your environment.

  Some are better layers, some more hardy. Check your local buy/swap/sell pages—often people give them away for free—or you can buy them from between $520 a hen, or rescue them from battery farms. Think carefully before you add a rooster to the mix. Not only will he love to sing you (and your poor neighbours) awake at 4 a.m., but your egg production may drop due to broody chooks. On the plus side, you will have chickens you can raise and either keep or sell, so just see what fits you best.

  You can also rent your chickens out. Yup, you read that right. Schools and daycares, families with young children, and people wanting to try chickens out but not sure they want to take the leap, could all potentially rent your hens. Renting 2 hens, a coop and their food for 4 weeks could net you around $150!

  Did I mention you'll never have to pay for eggs again?

Grab a pen and paper and brainstorm as many ideas as you can think of that would work in your unique situation while they are still fresh in your mind.

Do this for at least 10 minutes. Even if you can't think of anything after 1 minute, often if you persist you'll get a lot more ideas.

Write randomly and don't worry about spelling or full sentences or whether it makes sense or would work, just jot down whatever comes into your head.

You can go over your list later and refine what would work and is feasible. You might start by implementing one or two ideas, adding a few more as you can, or swapping them out where they don't work. The important thing is to start.

Key points:

- There are hundreds of options for making money on the side. You just have to find some that work for you. Brainstorm everything you can do to earn some extra cash.

- Work smarter—not harder!

- Start by implementing one moneymaking idea, and others as you can.

These are some of the more noteworthy tips for increasing your income enough to save a deposit and get your foot in the door. Before you have a conniption about all the debt that's holding you back, check out the next Chapter, *Breaking Free of Debt*. It leads you through what debt is and how it's changed over the decades, why you should pay off debt, and how to do it!

CHAPTER 4
BREAKING FREE OF DEBT

"The only way you will ever permanently take control of your financial life is to dig deep and fix the root problem."—

Suze Orman

Debt—the good, the bad and the ugly

Debt. One of the ugliest words I know.

No one wants it, everyone feels they 'need' it, and we just can't wait to be free of it.

In our grandparents' day there wasn't nearly so much of it. The cost of living helped. Enormously.

We're going to look at the 'median multiple' to show you how much harder paying off a mortgage is now than ever before. Put simply, the median multiple is this: the average house price divided by gross annual average household income. This means if you're going it alone it's even worse.

Housing affordability

In 2014, a Housing Affordability Study[15] ranked the top 9 metropolitan markets from 'affordable' through to 'severely

---

15
http://www.macrobusiness.com.au/2014/01/2014demographia-housing-affordability-survey

unaffordable' based on a house price to income ratio index. Australia was ranked 3rd worst, behind only Hong Kong and New Zealand, and was cited as being 'severely unaffordable!'

The United States was ranked the most affordable on a national scale of developed countries and even it was marked as 'moderately unaffordable!' These statistics are based on median figures nationwide, so even though America's East and West coasts are brutally unaffordable, the rest of the country evens these stats out.

At the end of the 1950's, the median house price in Sydney was around $7,000 at a time when average earnings were about $2,000 a year. The Ahuri Research Paper [16] on housing affordability in Australia gave it a 3-1 ratio. Now? The median house price in Sydney just smashed through the million-dollar mark, with an average wage of only $81,000. That puts the house price—income ratio today at 12.3—1.

This means it would take the average household their combined income for 12.3 years to pay a mortgage, more than four times as long as our grandparents.

In the United States, even after the housing collapse, an average home still costs 3 times as much as an average home in the 1970's, compared to the wage a person was earning at the time.

And yet Demographia[17] ranks the United States as the most affordable housing among the major metropolitan markets! What does that say about the rest of the world?

Furthermore, The Simple Dollar[18] found that a student in the

---

[16] http://www.ahuri.edu.au/downloads/publications/EvRevReports/NRV3_Research_Paper_10.pdf
[17] http://www.demographia.com/dhi.pdf
[18] http://www.thesimpledollar.com/a.dose-of-financial-reality

1970's could have worked part time at minimum wage (around 14 hrs) to pay their way through college. Now, students earning minimum wage would have to work full time (around 35 hrs) to pay their way. So their choice is to either be in debt or not attend college. Some choice!

So we've established that debt is not entirely as unavoidable as it was in the 50's. However, on the flip side, I think there is also a propensity to use this as an out. "I can't afford to buy a house." "It's not my fault." "I just don't earn enough." "How can I ever save a deposit?"

Our grandparents certainly weren't handed their homes. They still worked their butts off to buy them and we could learn some valuable lessons from them.

They took whatever jobs were available. They weren't too good to stack shelves, do manual labour, or work beneath bosses they hated. They didn't mind starting with what they could afford and working their way up to what they wanted!

They put in the time, put food on the table, saved, and paid off their mortgages. People were more resourceful. They made things, they made do, and they did things themselves. More of their pay check stayed in their pockets because of this.

It's not rocket science, people! We just have to be a little smarter nowadays.

Of course this is all just a broad generalisation of the decades, but debt is a little like the devil. If it doesn't get you one way, you can bet your bottom dollar it will try another route.

College degrees, 'interest-free' finance for cars, furniture, and holidays, Lay-By, credit cards, data plans for phones and tablets, personal loans—the list is endless.

What is debt?

When you are looking at buying a house, the first thing the banks look at is all of your current outgoings—your debt and your bills.

They affect how much you can borrow, how fast you can pay back your loan, and your ability to save.

The biggest forms of these are:

1. Credit cards!

2. Personal loans

3. Student loans

4. Monthly direct debits for memberships and subscriptions

5. Interest-free finance deals

6. Bills—power, water and insurance etc.

7. Living expenses—groceries and petrol etc.

All of these count against you when you're trying to get a mortgage. Not only this, but they severely limit your ability to save and pay off your mortgage quicker.

When debt can be good

If you have never had a credit card, look at signing up for one. While always paying cash for everything is an admirable trait, it leaves you with no credit record. If you pay for everything on a credit card but pay the balance off each month, then companies are able to see your spending. This gives you a better credit rating than someone who doesn't use a credit card at all.

It's backwards, I know, but that's just the way the system works, and you have to roll with it.

Other types of 'good' debt are an investment property that is lowering your tax bracket or a small business that is running at a 'loss' even while staying afloat, due to being able to claim many things others can't at the end of the tax year.

Getting rid of it

Before you get your mortgage you have three solutions for your debt.

1. Pay it off

Pour all your money into your debt, starting with the one with the highest interest rate, and GET RID OF IT!

This is what I think of as the best option.

You can use the budgeting step in *Chapter 1* to knock off debt, save for a deposit, or pay off a mortgage. The process is the same for all 3.

The lower your debt, the more you should focus on getting rid of it—it will only get bigger with interest, and none of the other options really apply for small debts.

Once your debt is gone you can focus on saving a deposit and buying a house.

Lenders will look on you much more kindly if you don't have any debt, and when you do have a mortgage, you can direct more of your money into it sooner, which will save you tens of thousands in the long run. Literally.

2. Consolidate your debt

If you know that your debt will never get paid off unless it is direct debited out of your bank account, or you get flustered trying to deal with multiple bills each month, then look at consolidation.

Google 'debt consolidation' and you will get hit with a stack of companies eager to help you out. Why? The interest they stand to earn on your loan. They might be saving you money, but don't kid yourself, they are in it for a reason too, and it isn't the good karma.

Debt consolidation is great for people who have a lot of different types and amounts of debts rather than just a few small ones to pay off.

It basically works by grouping all your debts into one, making them easier to manage. Usually, you can also obtain a lower interest rate than what you're paying.

Obviously, the length of the loans and the interest rates below are indicative only, they vary vastly from country to country, but here's an example for you:

You have 8 different forms of debt. The flat screen TV and the Lounge suite were both purchased with an interest-free finance deal that is due to run out. The other loans are all accruing interest already.

Type of loan	Cost	Interest	Length of loan
Car loan	$18,000	6%	10 years
Lounge suite	$3,800	14%	2 years after interest free
Credit card	$2,500	12%	Unlimited time
Credit card	$10,000	18%	Unlimited time
Credit card	$1,200	16%	Unlimited time
Student loan	$18,000	7%	Unlimited time
Personal loan-holiday	$10,000	15%	5 years
Flat screen TV	$4,000	14%	2 years after interest-free
	$67,500 TOTAL		

These give you a total of $67,500 in debt. Holy crap! You owe $67,500!! Just kidding. (-:

Seriously though—that's bad and you need to get rid of it. If you scraped together $740 per week to pay off your debts and set yourself a 2-year time frame to be debt free, this is what your minimum repayments and interest amounts would look like.

Type of loan	Loan amount	Time at minimum payment	Total paid
Credit card #1 18% Interest	$10,000	$117- minimum payment- 2 years	$12,165
Credit card #2 16% Interest	$1,200	$16- minimum payment- 2 years	$1,644
Personal loan 15% Interest	$10,000	$114- minimum payment- 2 years	$11,829
Lounge Suite 14% Interest	$3,800	$44- minimum payment- 2 years	$4,602
Flat screen TV 14% Interest	$4,000	$46- minimum payment- 2 years	$4,831
Credit card #3 12% Interest	$2500	$29- minimum payment- 2 years	$3,055
Student Loan 7% Interest	$18,000	$188- minimum payment- 2 years	$19,541
Car loan 6% Interest	$18,000	$186- minimum payment- 2 years	$19,352
TOTALS	**$67,500- TOTAL DEBT**	**$740 per week- MINIMUM PAYMENT 2 YEARS**	**$77,019- TOTAL PAID IN 2 YEARS**

So over 2 years you have paid an extra $10,000 in interest. This isn't as bad as it could be though. Spread these same debts out over a 10-year period and you would pay $120,693. Almost twice your original debt. Bottom line is—interest payments on debt are lethal!

Let's imagine you choose a debt consolidation company called Debt-Rid (purely fictional) to help you consolidate your loans. They are offering interest rates of 10% for the life of your loan.

Your student loan and car loan have lower interest rates, but the three credit cards, personal loan, and the TV and furniture loans are all higher. Debt-Rid sets up a loan of $31,500 and you pay off all your loans. Woo-hoo!

Except now you owe Debt-Rid $31,500. How is this any better?

Simply put, you will be paying less interest (if you did your research and picked a good one), and as your debts are all in one place they are much easier to keep track of and pay.

You are now left with only 3 monthly bills. As you can see the total is the same—you haven't actually paid any of your debt off, just consolidated it into fewer loans.

Type of Loan	Cost	Interest	Length of Loan
Car loan	$18,000	6%	10 years
Student loan	$18,000	7%	Unlimited time
Debt-rid loan	$31,500	10%	2 years
	$67,500		

Now your debt is consolidated, pay the minimum amount required on the car and student loans, and pour all your extra cash into paying off the Debt Rid loan, as this has the highest interest and will cost you the most in the long run. Once this is gone, tackle the student loan and then the car loan. OR take those 2 loans with you into a mortgage, if you feel you just really need to buy. But I still recommend you pay them off first.

As with your mortgage, always check to make sure there are no fees attached to your loans for paying them off fast. You don't want to do all that work only to be hit with massive fees! Make sure you choose a debt consolidation service that either doesn't have early repayment fees or would be happy to waive them.

Type of Loan	Weekly amount 1	Weekly amount 2	Weekly amount 3	Total paid
	1 year 2 months	5 months	4 months	
Debt-rid 10% Interest	$578 (maximum you can afford)	-PAID-	-PAID-	$33,131
Student loan 7% Interest	$82 (minimum payment)	$660 ($578+$82)	-PAID-	$19,375
Car loan 6% interest	$80 minimum payment	Maintain $80	$740 ($578+$82 +$80)	$19,580
	$740 total each week	**$740 total each week**	**$740 total each week**	**$72,086**

This is a rough estimate of how your repayments would look. Total paid over all debts was $72,086 and it took under 2 years to get yourself debt free. This is based on a large debt, however. Not all debts will take this long or cost this much to be free of. Notice that the total amount paid is $5,000 less with debt consolidation than without?

3. Add to your debts

If your debts are too large and will take years to pay off even when throwing everything at them, or if you live in an area where house prices just keep increasing and you need to get on the ladder NOW, then look at adding to your debt with a home loan. I know, I know, WTF, right!?

The pros are obvious. You're on the property ladder, you've got a home, and you're living the dream.

But! (There's always a but.) You're also going to end up paying so much more for your mortgage in the long run because you simply don't have enough money to be paying double payments.

Remember all those other debts? Yeah, they're still there, and you still need to pay them off every month too.

Your debt will ensure you miss those critical first years and any mortgage payments you make will be just like every other schmuck: Pretty much worthless.

So why is this an option? Mostly because it gets you on the property ladder sooner, and if you were honest with yourself and bought because your local area was sky-rocketing, you may find yourself sitting on a home with great equity, without having paid off a cent.

Our home is worth twice today what we paid for it 10 years ago—through no work of our own. If this happens, then a seemingly stupid move can become an awesome one.

Key points:

- Debt is much harder to escape today than ever before, but that doesn't mean it's completely unavoidable.

- Debt is anything you owe money on such as credit cards, personal loans, and memberships.

- Paying debt off early is the best option.

- Paying debt off fast will save you big money in the long run.

Debt is a hard thing to get rid of, but without it, paying off your mortgage will be much less stressful and a much quicker process. If you are having trouble getting your head around your bills, interest rates, and finances, book yourself in with a financial planner and let them do the legwork. The few hundred you pay them will be worth it to sort yourself out.

Still with me? Deep breath and dive into the next chapter, where we work out how much you can borrow, your weekly repayments, and all the things that make up *The Magic Formula*.

CHAPTER 5
THE MAGIC FORMULA

"Success occurs when opportunity meets preparation."—
Zig Ziglar

Every book needs a magic formula!

Understanding and following this formula will give you a better grasp on the subjects discussed later in the book and will help jump start your efforts to succeed and become mortgage free in the shortest possible space of time.

So here it is—the magic formula:

Spend less to pay off more.

Ground-breaking, right? I'm sure your little world has been rocked by such an earth-shattering revelation. Spend less to pay off more? That's it?

Of course that's not it!

Hang in there, and I will walk you through the whole process.

Borrowing power

When you first visit a bank with an eye to getting a mortgage, the first thing they will do is figure out how much you can borrow. You can do this yourself from home too, with an aptly named 'borrowing power' calculator. Just Google and go!

Both the banks and the calculators will require you to show how much money you earn, how much you pay in bills, how much is owing on credit cards and finance deals and any outstanding debts you may have.

You will also need to indicate your marital status, and if you have any dependent children.

Keep all the stock figures in place. So, if your bank has a current interest rate of 6%, a 30-year loan is the norm, and payments are made monthly, then just roll with that. Once completed, your borrowing power calculation will give you an indication of what the *bank* thinks you can borrow.

Write down your figure and what the interest rate, loan term, and repayment frequencies were, and move on.

Extra repayments calculator

I love this calculator. It's another great one to Google and will show you how much interest and time you will save on your loan with added payments.

It is especially useful for people who have already bought their home, or for anyone trying to get their head around just how much the extra repayments will save them.

Make the calculator work for you. If you want to know how many years you can pay your loan off in, fill out the usual parameters and then your proposed extra payments. Have a look at the graph at the bottom and it will show you exactly how much time and money you will save. Super cool.

Double trouble

Essentially, to pay off your house in a third of the time as your peers, you have two options. Either pay double mortgage payments, or buy a cheaper home.

If you haven't bought yet, you can use the borrowing power calculations to make sure you buy a house cheaply enough to pay it off in the time you want.

Check out the graph below. The amount at the bottom shows the weekly repayment on a 30-year mortgage (the blue bar). The red bar shows how much you could actually afford to buy a home for, if you wanted to maintain the same payments, but pay it off in 10 years. The purple bar is your middle ground. It is what I call your 'true mortgage amount.'

Calculate your true mortgage amount by taking your weekly repayment and adding 20%. This 20% is made up of savings from tightening your belt, making extra money, and saving more. You might find you can add even more. The figure varies from person to person. The aim is to pay off as much as you can on the smallest loan you can get.

WEEKLY PAYMENTS AND LOAN AMOUNT

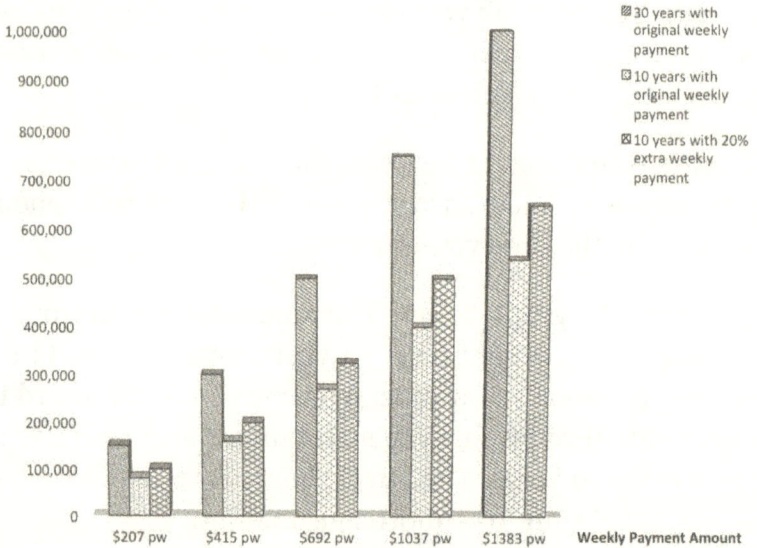

Legend:
- 30 years with original weekly payment
- 10 years with original weekly payment
- 10 years with 20% extra weekly payment

Y-axis: 0, 100,000, 200,000, 300,000, 400,000, 500,000, 600,000, 700,000, 800,000, 900,000, 1,000,000

X-axis (Weekly Payment Amount): $207 pw, $415 pw, $692 pw, $1037 pw, $1383 pw

If you have already bought your home and want to pay it off in 10 years, you will need to pay double. It is not necessarily double. Depending on the amount of the mortgage it can work out to just over half again. But it is a lot more than you're currently paying.

Apply everything in this book to your advantage to get those extra payments happening. Cut your excesses, write a kick-arse budget, and learn how to make some extra moola.

Work with an 'extra repayments calculator' online and see how much extra you are going to need to pay each week.

Because you are shifting so much mortgage interest with your extra repayments, they not only pay off your loan 20 years sooner, but also save you a shed load of money!

What you actually want to be borrowing

The simplest way for you to see how much you can actually afford to spend on a house is to pull up any 'loan repayment calculator' on the net. Plug in the figures you wrote down previously, what the *banks* think you can spend at their current interest rate, with a monthly repayment and a 30-year mortgage.

This figure is what most people base their house purchases on. Based on a $500,000 mortgage, I would have a monthly repayment of $2,998, and a total interest amount of $579,191 over the life of the loan.

LOAN AMOUNT	MONTHLY PAYMENT WITH 6% INTEREST	INTEREST OVER LOAN LIFE	TOTAL COST OF LOAN
$150,000	$900	$173,758	$323,758
$300,000	$1799	$347,515	$647,515
$500,000	$2,998	$579,191	$1,079,191
$750,000	$4,497	$868,787	$1,618,787
$1,000,000	$5,996	$1,158,382	$2,158,382

Now begin your changes. I will go through the why's of each of these things next.

Change the loan term to 10 years.

Change the interest rate to 2% more than the current rate.

Change the monthly payments to weekly.

Changing the $500,000 loan to an 8% interest rate and implementing the other changes, I get a weekly repayment of $1,398! This is $6058 a month. Over twice what the bank deems I am able to repay! Did you note the difference in interest payments over the life of the loan though? Less than half what it was. Not only are you saving 20 years, but $352,433! For most people, paying double is out of the question though.

LOAN AMOUNT	WEEKLY PAYMENT WITH 8% INTEREST	INTEREST OVER LOAN LIFE	TOTAL COST OF LOAN
$150,000	$420/ $1820 monthly	$68,028	$218,028
$300,000	$839/ $3,635 monthly	$136,055	$436,055
$500,000	$1,398/ $6058 monthly	$226,758	$726,758
$750,000	$2,097/ $9,082 monthly	$340,137	$1,090,137
$1,000,000	$2,796/ $12,116 monthly	$453,515	$1,453,515

Start playing around with the amount. If you are like us, you know that you can save more than what the bank thinks. Others will find it's about right. Use your budget from *Chapter 1* and the money saving and money making techniques from *Chapters 2* and *4*, to get an accurate figure on how much you have to spend. Not just for a bit—for 10 years!

If I stuck to the $2,998 the bank thinks I could repay each month, I would only be able to borrow around $230,000 and still be able to pay off my loan in 10 years.

That's a far cry from half a million! I know I can save more though, let's say $3,900 a month. That gives me my 'True mortgage amount' of $300,000. Let me show you.

	BANK MORTGAGE	NEW MORTGAGE	TRUE MORTGAGE
Mortgage amount	$500,000	$230,000	$300,000
Loan term	30 Years	10 Years	10 Years
Interest rate	6%	8%	8%
Payment amount	$2,998 paid monthly ($692 a week)	$698 paid weekly ($3,023 a month)	$910 paid weekly ($3943 a month)
Interest over life of loan	$579,191	$91,148	$118,889
Total cost of loan	$1,079,191	$321,148	$418,889

As you can see, both the bank mortgage and the new mortgage have a repayment amount of around $3,000 a month. My true mortgage has a repayment of $3,943 because I was able to cut back on spending and make some money on the side. I put all this 'extra' money into making bigger repayments. This allows me to borrow more, while still paying off my mortgage in 10 years.

The dollar amount you come up with using this formula is your true figure.

It's probably really disheartening and not what you want to see at all—especially compared to the first 'bank figures' you worked out—but if you want to pay your home loan off in 10 years you have to be realistic.

Is it awful? Yes. Heart breaking? Probably. Will you be ahead of the curve and able to spend more in 10 years' time? Most definitely! Sometimes to get ahead you have to dial back, and this is one of those times.

This figure might change as you implement some of the ideas found in *Mortgage Free*. You may be able to make great cuts and utilise some awesome moneymaking techniques that make it possible to save more. So I would encourage you to revisit this chapter once you have soaked up every bit of information you can.

Loan term

Why 10 years? It doesn't have to be! But I am using 10 years as a starting point because I think it's an attainable figure for most people. You might be able to pay it off in12 years, 5 years or even 3! If you think you've got what it takes to do this, then just replace 10 years with your desired figure every time I talk about it and the maths will do the rest.

You don't need to change the length of your mortgage to 10 years when setting it up, or refinance to a shorter term. In fact, I would recommend leaving your mortgage length at 30 years. That way if you have any difficulties later on you will not need to refinance. Paying extra repayments will do the same job as setting your loan to a shorter term to begin with.

Repayment frequency

Why weekly or fortnightly? You get paid monthly and it's easier for you to pay your mortgage when your pay comes in. In the first few months this might actually be true, but considering you can set up direct debits and separate accounts, this really doesn't make any difference. Making your payments weekly or fortnightly is the single easiest thing you can do to save time and money on your mortgage.

Why? There are 12 months in a year (kinda hope you knew that), so if you pay your mortgage monthly, you make 12 repayments. When paying fortnightly you are paying half as much each time, but instead of making 24 repayments (12x2) you are making 26 (the number of fortnights in a year). You are effectively paying a whole extra month of repayments every year by paying fortnightly or weekly, and yet you don't really notice. Check this out.

Take a look at the next graph. Our $500,000 mortgage example paid monthly will end up costing you $579,191 in interest over the life of the loan (dear Lord, that's horrendous!). Paying fortnightly will take it down to $455,131. Paying weekly only drops a tiny bit extra bringing it to $454,581, but every little bit helps, right?

So paying weekly instead of monthly will save you a whopping $124,610 over the life of your loan as well as 5½ years; over 120 grand just for changing your payment frequency. Equal parts awesome and easy! This is the number one thing you can do to pay off your mortgage faster.

PAYMENT FREQUENCY

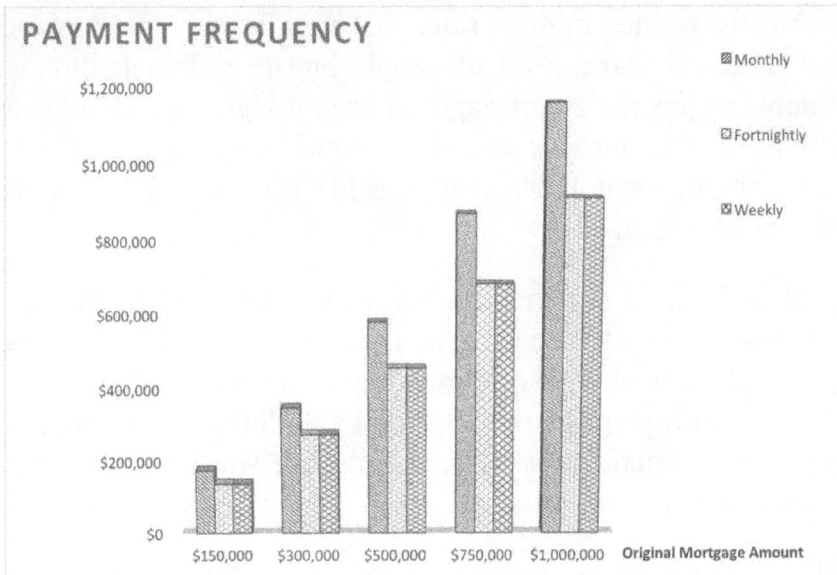

Interest rate

Why do we increase the interest rate by 2-5%? When you are making extra repayments you have the ability to set and forget. In short, you can specify a dollar figure, greater than your minimum repayments, that gets direct debited from your account each week, and not change it again for 10 years.

If you are on a fixed rate you do this anyway, but at the minimum required amount. If you are on a variable rate, the amount will change month to month based on its length and any interest rate changes. Setting a figure higher than your minimum repayments ensures you know exactly how much is outgoing each month and ensures you are paying as much as possible without 'forgetting' to.

Interest rates vary over time, sometimes by a little, sometimes by a lot. By giving yourself a 2-5% 'buffer' you don't have to change your direct debit amount every time the interest rate changes.

In the 90's, when interest rates in Australia and New Zealand hit the 20% mark, a lot of people had to sell their homes, unable to pay their mortgages at such a high rate. By adding 5% to the current rate you give yourself a fighting chance to stay afloat, even if (heaven forbid) the interest rates do skyrocket again.

Take a look at the interest rates and see what people are predicting will happen with the rates in the near future. If you can't afford to add 5% on interest and the rates look stable or in a downward spiral, then just add 2%. This is up to you, and while not strictly necessary, it can save you both time and money in the long run.

If you don't mind changing direct debits as interest rates change, then by all means just start with the going rate. But always work out what you can afford based on more. Sometimes an interest rate change of just 2% can mean the difference between maintaining double payments or not.

You do not want to jeopardise your ten-year plan because of an interest rate hike.

Keep it simple, stupid

As you can see, the magic formula is super simple. Spend less to pay off more.

Work out how much you need to repay each week to pay off your mortgage in the time you want, and then set out and make it happen.

If you've already bought a house, then utilise the information provided to make more money, save more money, and make extra repayments.

If you have yet to buy, then it's even easier. You can start off right by buying a house that fits your budget and your time frame.

Key points:

- Spend less to pay off more.

- Utilise mortgage calculators to help work out your actual borrowing power.

- Always set your repayments to weekly or fortnightly.

- Make sure you leave an interest buffer in case rates rise.

- Use the resources in the following chapters to help you with extra payments.

Whatever stage you're at, remember that the sooner you start, the bigger the difference it will make to your bank balance and your life. Up next we cover mortgage brokers, bank fees, preapprovals and so much more! All these are key to *Finding a Good Bank and a Great Mortgage.*

CHAPTER 6
FINDING A GOOD BANK AND A GREAT MORTGAGE

"A bank is a place that will lend you money if you can prove that you don't need it."—Bob Hope

Finding a good bank

Choosing a bank can be the hardest part of getting your mortgage. Everyone is trying to out-do themselves and sign you up with their latest and greatest deal. Why? Because the interest you pay on your loan makes their world go round. Just remember that they need you more than you need them, and be prepared to ask the tough questions and do some bargaining.

Don't ignore the smaller or independent banks. Sometimes they have awesome deals, great interest rates, and fabulous customer service. Unlike the larger banks, they will be more interested in having you bank with them, and are often more answerable to their clientele, pushing through reforms and dropping rates much quicker than other banks. We went with a small local bank and they have been fabulous.

Ask your mates. Ask your work colleagues. Ask your family. Don't just take the banks' word for how amazing they are—ask around. Word of mouth is a powerful tool, as it doesn't just see the facts and figures. It shows a broader view of the bank from their customer service, to how easily you can make revisions, how quick they are to offer help, act on reserve bank rate changes, and just generally how they are to work with.

You don't have to request specifics. Just ask people who they bank with and if they are happy with them. If you know them a bit better, you could also ask if there are specific things they do or don't do well.

Print off our Mortgage Check-list[19] and go through it with your broker or your bank. Here are some ideas to help you pick the right bank and an awesome mortgage.

Mortgage brokers

A mortgage broker helps you get the most out of your loan. They know the banks, what they offer, and what deals are currently available. They can be a valuable asset when you're looking for a great mortgage.

They can also be a massive liability. Not every broker is as good at their job as the next one. Try to get a referral, and if you feel they are not up to scratch, go with someone else. Getting the right mortgage is one of the most important things you will do, so make sure your broker is worth their salt. They will generally cost you a few hundred, although some are free as they rely on a commission from your chosen bank.

- Do your homework. Does the mortgage broker only represent certain banks? Many do, and you could be missing out on a better deal by a bank they are not giving you information on.

- Don't kid yourself—unless you get a truly exceptional broker, most will be happy to get you 4 out of the 10

---

[19] http://www.how2without.com/bonus-materials/mortgage-free-workbook/

things you were looking for in a mortgage for a higher referral fee. Make sure they not only know what you want, but don't accept anything less. Be specific!

- Let them do the legwork. This is their job and something they are good at (you'd hope!)

- Listen! Again, this is their field, and they may have some really great information to offer. If you aren't going to take on any advice, perhaps look into the banks yourself.

- If you think your mortgage broker isn't doing a great job, get another one or do the legwork yourself. Personally, I wish I had just done things myself. While I was happy with the bank I got, our mortgage broker was beyond useless; I still ended up working out figures, fees, and other issues. This is not true of all brokers, as there are some great ones out there.

- Again, ask around. As with finding a bank, word of mouth is the best place to find competent and knowledgeable brokers.

- Use this feedback, and compare it to what your broker is telling you. They are viewing banks purely by what is on paper, whereas customers are viewing them by experience. The two can be very different.

- A mortgage broker could be invaluable if you are a 'high risk' client. This could include self-employed people, those with a bad credit rating, and those with low income. Brokers know which banks are more likely to accept your application and what extra paperwork you require. They can also help by recommending ways to clean up your credit rating.

Bank fees

Bank fees. Bleugh! They are one of those unavoidable things when getting a mortgage, but some are definitely worse than others.

- Application or pre-approval fee. Banks sometimes charge these fees for a 'pre-approved' loan to 'hold' the money for you while you're looking at properties. There is more information on pre-approvals later in this chapter.

- Sign-up fee. These can be hundreds of dollars and are charged by the bank because of all the work related to setting up your new loan. Sometimes a bank will waive the fee to encourage you to take up their loan offer. Always ask them to!

- Valuation fee. These are charged for the banks assessor to do a basic walk-through of your proposed property, so they can confirm your property is worth what you're paying for it. They often don't agree with the real estate agents' figures.

- Maintenance fees. These are usually monthly and charged by the bank to 'maintain' your loan. They are not normally much—around $5-$20 a month. Some banks don't charge them, and others only charge them on some plans.

- Breaking a fixed rate. This is one you normally can't get waived. If you sign up to a fixed rate at 7% and the rates drop to 4%, you're going to be kicking yourself and wanting out. However, the fees might be so high it's not worth it. Do your math and see if you should stick it out or pay the fee.

- Lenders mortgage insurance or higher lending charge. LMI or HLC is a type of insurance that credit providers take out to protect themselves from

  borrowers not being able to repay the loan. It is normally charged for loans where you borrow more than 80% of the property's value. See *Chapter 7* for more information.

- The same is true of the Extra repayment fee. Banks don't want you to pay off your loan fast—it's bad for their back pockets. To compensate themselves for your awesomeness they charge you a fee to make extra payments. Make sure this is not attached to any loan you choose to get!

- Redraw fee. You shouldn't be redrawing anyway, but if you do need to, you definitely don't want to be paying a fee to access your own money. Check it out.

- Direct debit fee. Some banks have the hide to try and charge you for each direct debit to your account. Remember how we talked about payment frequency and how paying weekly could save you $100,000 in interest over the life of your loan? Well, the banks want that $100 grand, and so they hope when a client sees a fee each time they make a payment, they will stick with monthly payments instead of weekly. Super cheeky.

- Own building insurance fee. If you have a mortgage, then you are also required by the bank to have property insurance to protect their investment. This fee is charged if you decide to take out insurance with anyone other than your bank. Rude.

- Refinancing fee. Has the deal you signed up for run out, or is another bank offering better value?

Refinancing fees encourage you not to look for better deals by charging an exorbitant fee for refinancing—even within the same bank.

- Exit fee or break cost. This is charged if you exit your loan before it runs its course (the length it was drawn

  up for). If you have a 30-year loan that you plan on paying off in 10 years, or if your bank is terrible and you decide to swap to another one, you could be hit with thousands of dollars in fees. Not only is this horrendous, but it is also totally unavoidable. If your favourite bank has this on all their loans, ask them to waive it, or pick another bank. There is no point paying off your mortgage super-fast if you are then punished for doing so.

For any of these fees, ask. If you have a mortgage broker, make one of your stipulations be for no extra repayment or exit fees and as few other fees as possible. If you are doing it all yourself, pit the banks against each other. Find your top 3 banks and see what all their fees are and what, if any, deals they have.

Sit down with each bank and let them know you are looking at their bank in conjunction with several others and that it has really come down to the fees charged.

See what they come up with.

Most banks won't charge all of these fees, and in some countries they don't even exist, so just suss out what is pertinent for you and do the best you can.

Banks make so much money in interest over the life of an average loan they are normally very keen to play ball when it comes to signing up a new client. Not only will a good bank be happy to spend time walking you through their different loans; you will probably find they will waive a considerable amount to sign you on. Once locked into a mortgage, you will probably find banks won't be as accommodating to change, so make sure you check all the fees first—not later.

The most important charges to avoid will always be the extra repayment fees and the early exit fees. These are nonnegotiable when paying off your mortgage fast.

Take the Mortgage Checklist[20] with you when speaking to banks. It will provide you with a list of questions to ask at every step.

Getting a great mortgage

Once you've got your bank lined up, choose your mortgage. There are some really simple things you can do when setting up your mortgage that will immediately catapult you ahead of the game. Make sure you talk to the bank about anything you don't like.

Some banks will change things for you if you complain!

Pre-approval

Before you even hit the open homes this weekend, get yourself a pre-approval. Getting pre-approval can be the difference between bagging the property you want and someone else getting it first. They have become part of almost every real estate deal and let the seller know you're serious; it also gives you a firm figure with which to bid on properties. What are they? The name kind of says it all. It is the bank's word that

---

[20] http://www.how2without.com/bonus-materials/mortgage-free-workbook/

they will give you a loan for a certain amount of money. You don't have the loan yet; it is just 'approved.'

Once you know which bank you want to use, take in your paperwork and have a sit down with them. They will need to see:

- Proof of income.

- Proof of deposit (savings).

- Proof of monthly outgoings such as bills, credit cards, and loans.

You know, all the normal stuff.

As long as you meet their requirements, you will then have a pre-approved mortgage and will be free to house hunt for the perfect home. A pre-approval is normally valid for 3-6 months, at which point you would have to apply again.

Be aware, though, that just because a bank has pre-approved your loan doesn't mean they will give you one. You what now?! I know, doesn't make sense, right?

When you get pre-approval, a loan officer usually issues it, but it has not been through the whole loan process of being underwritten by trained officers, and as such, may still be turned down right when you need it.

Your best defence against this happening is to be as open and honest with the bank as possible. If there are things you don't tell them when you go for pre-approval, the underwriter will find them when it's crunch time, and it could be something that makes your loan unfavourable enough to turn down.

The bank will look at all your paperwork again once it's time to issue the loan, so if it takes you 5 months to find a property and your circumstances have changed in that space of time, or if the lender thinks you've paid more for the property than what it's worth, then you could be in for an unpleasant surprise.

If your circumstances do change, make sure they don't affect your credit rating or your income source. If you're worried, go back to the bank and get them to do another pre-approval.

Remember, these should be at no obligation and should cost you nothing—any loan fees are generally paid once the mortgage has settled.

Repayment frequency

We covered this in *Chapter Five*: Weekly or fortnightly. Do not make monthly repayments! I forbid it!

Interest rates

Shop around and see which bank has cheaper interest rates. While 'honeymoon' rates (usually for the first year of the loan) are great, remember to check the rate after the special has finished. Remember, you have 10 years to get through, not just one!

Also check out statistics on Google, and see whether banks are fast or slow to raise and lower interest rates after reserve bank changes are announced.

Variable or Fixed

When we bought our first home, we asked for advice from a friend of ours, a wily Maltese/Australian gent called Leo who had been in the banking industry for 30-odd years. One of the things he had to convince us on was going with a variable rate.

Being the cautious people we are, we were going to get a fixed rate as it gave us the certainty of knowing that the interest rate wouldn't jump through the roof and have us paying heaps more, and we would always know what we were paying each month.

Leo told us after his years of banking he would always recommend the variable rate. Fixed rates are usually set quite a bit higher than variable so the banks don't lose money if rates do jump. Leo postulated that any benefits you may have gained by having a fixed rate when interest rates are rising are completely negated by the extra you pay at the beginning when interest rates are lower.

The first few years of a home loan are the most critical, and higher interest rates then can really hurt it in the long run.

And he was right. We took the variable and have always been glad we did. Our rates were lower in the beginning, and when the rates started dropping we watched friends with fixed mortgages anguish about how much less they would be paying if their rate hadn't been fixed.

Don't get me wrong; we got lucky. There are no two ways about it. We had reasonable rates at the onset of our loan and they only got lower from there. You may not be as lucky. However, if you add your buffer in, you should come out the other side smelling of roses. Oh, and if the interest rates are kind to you, that buffer will help you pay off your loan even sooner. (-:

This rule of thumb works really well in Australia, as our fixed rates are higher than our variable. In New Zealand, however, fixed rates are lower than variable rates to encourage you to lock in loan terms with your bank. If this is the case in your country, look at what the differences between the two are, and whether the rates are tipped to go up or down, and make a decision accordingly.

Redraw facility

Redraw. Something that gets a lot of homeowners into strife. It is often viewed as 'free money' or 'savings,' and in some ways this is true, but only while it stays on your loan.

What is it? A redraw facility essentially keeps track of any extra payments you've made over the life of your loan and allows you to use that money or 'redraw' it from your mortgage account.

For example, if your minimum repayment is $823 a week, but you pay in $1,323, then $500 a week would sit in your redraw account. While there, it works as though it has paid off your mortgage and lowers the interest rates. Once you draw it out, the interest portion of your loan goes up to reflect the new loan balance. You with me?

Redraws or 'draw down facilities' have their advantages and their disadvantages. After a year of trying for our second, child we found out I had 'secondary infertility' and decided that we would redraw our mortgage to do IVF. We only redrew $20,000 and we were paying off around $43,000 a year at the time, but it added a whole year. Why? Because as soon as we redrew that money, we were paying more in interest and less off our principal. It makes a *huge* difference.

So here's my two cents' worth. We decided it was worth the cost of redrawing because having children was something we could only do for a finite period of time. You would need to make a similar assessment.

- Do you need the money for a health-related issue? This is something that is incredibly important, and the only thing I would consider using redraw for.
Totally worth it.

- Are you desperate for a holiday? Suck it up! There are many ways to have a fabulous holiday without redrawing your mortgage to do it. Just think, you can holiday anywhere in the world as soon as you've paid off your mortgage. Not worth it.

- You need a reliable car to get to work. If you can't take public transport or car pool with a colleague, then yes, you do. There is nothing worse than having car troubles. I know—I lived through 10 years of them! I was lucky, though. I had a husband who could fix almost everything, we had a second car, and I was within walking distance of public transport, shops, and schools. Not everyone is as fortunate.

  However, you don't have to buy a car straight off the showroom floor, or even a new second-hand one. There are some fabulous, reliable cars out there for a fraction of the amount of a new or near-new one, and they won't add a year to your mortgage. Try and borrow a friend's second car, or make do without one until you can save some money. If you do have to redraw, make sure it is as little as possible. Not worth it.

- Visiting family and friends. If you're like me and you live in a different country from that in which you were born, then visiting family may be a big deal for you. I know it is for us. And air travel is not cheap. At least not in this neck of the woods. Think, though, how often you could visit them once your mortgage is gone. You could even buy a holiday home. Travel is something you should save for, not redraw for. Not worth it.

- Upskilling yourself. Do you need money to attend a course or develop skills in your field? Really look at the end result. Will you receive a certificate for all your hard work and money, but no furtherance to your career? Or will that extra learning catapult you

  up a level and give you increased weekly earnings? Make sure you are going to be receiving more in increased earnings than what you paid out. Might be worth it.

- Do you want to do some renovations? They add value to your home anyway, right? Yes, some renovations do, and some don't (see *Chapter 9* for the 10 best and worst renovations). But no renovation adds enough to cover the cost of itself combined with the extra time and money you will add to your loan from redrawing for it. Learn to live with it until you can afford to change it. I lived without a kitchen for 3½ years, just cooking on a camp stove, although I did have a sink and running water, (held up by two sticks). And no, I wasn't young and at work all day.

One year into being kitchen-less I had a newborn baby and was home every day. You would be amazed at what you can get used to. Don't get me wrong, I was often embarrassed by my home when people visited, especially if they were new friends, but whenever I got down I would just remind myself that in a few years I could buy whatever I wanted.

And you know what, no one except me really cared anyway. I'm sure people thought we were nuts and that they wouldn't/couldn't live like that, but they didn't spend their lives obsessing over the state of my home. They had their own things to think about. Bottom line is, renovations are not worth redrawing for either.

I know all these things are incredibly important to different people for different reasons, but if you want them that badly, then save the money a different way. Start a coin jar or put aside $20 a week in a separate account. If you get the chance to do overtime or earn some money on the side, then save this and put it towards whatever you're hanging out for. Unless it is going to physically hurt you to not redraw, don't do it!

So should you even bother?

Unfortunately, life sometimes throws us curve balls. For us it was infertility. For others it might be the loss of a job without immediately being able to find another one. Some people might be struggling with a cancer diagnosis or have family in desperate need of help. This is where redraw is king. In situations like these, which, unlike the examples above, are forced on us instead of being chosen, the ability to redraw can make all the difference to survival.

If you can see $140,000 sitting in your redraw account and not touch it, then yes, I would recommend it. However, if money burns a hole in your pocket and the thought of all that money sitting there brings visions of palm trees and mojitos, then I would advise against it. If something terrible does happen (I truly hope it never does), then you can always refinance your mortgage, or get a personal loan. This may be a safer bet for you.

Offset account

An offset account is a bank account into which everything gets deposited: Your wages, your savings, and any extra money you get.

It operates in a similar way to a redraw facility, by lowering the interest portion of your loan based on how much is in your account on a daily basis.

Unlike a redraw account, it is a transaction account and is made to be used like one. You will have bank cards attached to it and be able to set up direct debits and make payments from it. This is something we would have loved as part of our mortgage and one of the things our broker stuffed up...

Offset accounts are great if you hold money in your account for monthly direct debits and bill payments. All of that money, while already earmarked for a particular purpose, is also lowering the interest portion of your loan. They are not as much use if you get paid and the money immediately leaves your account.

Refer back to this section or print off our Mortgage Checklist[21] when you begin visiting banks. This will help remind you what you want and need in a mortgage, without getting drowned in information!

Key Points:

- Repay your mortgage weekly or fortnightly. It is the easiest change with the biggest result you can make.

---

[21] http://www.how2without.com/bonus-materials/mortgage-free-workbook/

- Get a bank and a mortgage that will work for you, and with you, for the best results.

- Bank fees are often unavoidable, but ensure you never sign up for a loan that has exit or early repayment fees.

- Pre-approvals make buying much easier and let you know how much the banks will lend you ahead of time.

- Mortgage brokers can be fabulous, especially for high-risk applicants. Make sure you use word of mouth to find a good one.

I know it's a lot to take in, but getting a good bank and a great mortgage will make such a difference to your loan term! Use the resources, be assertive, and remember that the banks are benefiting from you, so don't feel bad for making them work hard!

Next up, in *Chapter 7: A Trick for Every Situation*, we look at tricky situations and how to get out of them alive! Are you partway through a mortgage? Taking a mortgage into retirement? A high-risk client? We cover them all!

CHAPTER 7
A TRICK FOR EVERY SITUATION

"When we are no longer able to change a situation, we are challenged to change ourselves."—Viktor E. Frankl

Already bought your property?

It is never too late to make positive changes to your mortgage term. Most of the chapters in Mortgage Free have a host of information that can still help you pay your mortgage off fast, even if you're partway through. Read through them and apply anything you can. Here are a few for now, though:

- Make sure your repayment frequency is set to fortnightly, not monthly. This is the single easiest thing you can do to pay off your mortgage faster.

- Follow the steps in *Chapter 1: Sustainable Budgeting* and make sure you know what you're spending where.

- Use *Chapters 2 and 3* to learn how to cut back, make more money, and save more.

- Use this 'extra' money to immediately start making additional mortgage repayments. The sooner you start topping up payments, the sooner you will see results.

- Check your mortgage against other service providers and make sure you are getting the best deal possible.

See *Chapter 6* for advice on banks, mortgages, and refinancing.

- Do not redraw unless something is time sensitive or someone is literally dying! Taking money from your mortgage adds much more time and money than you realise.

- The more repayments you make, the more they snowball, with the good effects becoming bigger and more noticeable over time. Keep at it!

If you want something a bit more precise than just paying extra payments, then do some figures. I would suggest doing your budget and following *Chapters 2-4* before tackling this.

If you suck at budgeting then take a look at my book *Brilliant Budgets and Despicable Debt.*[22] It will help you find and implement a budget that will work with you and your lifestyle.

A budget may be the last thing on your mind, but you will be amazed at how much you can scrape together each week by understanding your finances more, and what a big difference this extra cash can make to your repayments.

Once you know exactly how much money you can spare each week, take your current mortgage amount and plug it into a loan repayment calculator.

Now increase the interest rate to 2% more than the current rate, decrease the mortgage length to 10 years and make sure the repayment frequency is set to weekly, and the interest rate to variable. Slowly reduce or increase the loan length until you hit a repayment amount you think you can sustain.

---

22 https://www.amazon.com/Budget-mall-Change-Big-Reward-Book-ebook/dp/B01DXQT9LI

You don't have to refinance for this length of time, just pay the amount indicated, and it will still be paid off in the time you chose.

With a fixed goal now in mind you can start smashing your payments and know you'll be debt free in the time you allocated yourself.

That's a great feeling!

I'm retired. Will this work?

What about people who are further on in their life, who are almost at retirement or already retired, and not in a good place financially after marriage break-ups, business failures, or just bad management?

Can they still pay off their mortgage fast?

I said this book was relevant to everyone and I stand by that, but there are two sides to this question.

Is it possible? Yes, I think so. Should they? That is another question entirely.

When you're retired or close to it, the question should not be 'can you pay off your mortgage,' but 'should you?'

The benefits of paying off your house when you're younger are many and varied. You pay so much less in interest, you can do more without debt, you can look at buying subsequent houses for investment purposes, and so on. When you retire, many of these benefits go out the window.

You no longer have the years left to play around in the real estate game, and banks are often cautious about lending large sums of money to those who they see as about to drop dead. I mean, seriously—most retirees probably have another 30 years left in them, not to mention a fantastic grasp on saving and the value of a dollar. Ridiculous!

I think, like most things, being at the bottom or top end of the age spectrum always makes things more challenging. Generally, once you're of retirement age you have either given up work or are doing reduced hours. Many are living on their superannuation or government benefits. You just don't have the disposable income to throw at your mortgage that you did as a 30-year-old. You do, however, have more time than the average person.

Some of the money making and money saving tips in the first few chapters would be hard for those working full time to implement, but are perfect for those at home more often. Consider taking in boarders or using your home as a Bed and Breakfast. Grow fruit and veggies and sell what you don't use, raise chickens and sell the surplus eggs. Look through our list in *Chapter 3* and find anything you can, to help you get ahead. Then put your spare change in a jar and read on...

According to data from a 2013 Study [23], the median mortgage balance for those still paying off mortgages between the ages of 50 and 69 years is $118,000. They suggest that before rushing to pay off their home loans, these baby boomers should look to other things first.

- Make sure all high-interest credit cards are paid off every month

- Pay bills on time to keep up a good credit rating. (Limiting your credit use to 30% or less of what's available also helps credit scores.)

---

23 http://demandinstitute.org/baby-boomers-and-their-homes

- If you're still working, add money to your super and take advantage of tax breaks and government cocontributions that will boost your savings.

- Build your emergency funds. These can be in a savings account, or as cash under your mattress. Whatever works for you. An especially great way to save for emergencies is to make your redraw account your emergency funds, so that you are saving money on your mortgage interest at the same time.

There are also many other things open to people with little or no time left in the work force.

- Invest. For those with super or who are still working, it may be a better value to invest any spare money or super lump sums than to pay off your mortgage. If you can earn more off your investment than what your interest payments on the mortgage are, then this could be a viable option. On the other hand, if you have funds in a low-interest account that could pay off your high-interest mortgage, then that may work better for you.

- Downsize. Often older couples still have the large homes that they raised their children in. Selling the family home and downsizing not only makes sense financially, but is also a lot less effort and work to keep up as you get older.

- Equity. 9 times out of 10, the house you're sitting on will be worth considerably more now than when you bought it. You may have $118,000 left on your loan, but your home is worth half a million. That gives you around $380,000 in equity. If you don't want to sell up, consider buying an investment property and using the income from that to pay off first your home and then the investment property. Make sure you do your figures, though, and get it to work for you by being either positively geared or by making it that way through tax deductible expenses, etc. *(see Chapter 12)*.

- Income tax deductions. Living in America? You might be eligible for a tax break if you hold onto your mortgage. If this is you, then it may make more sense to build up your savings for retirement than to pay off a low-interest mortgage.

- You might need funds to tap into. Paying off your mortgage and then not having enough for medical or living expenses is just plain crazy. Make sure if you are paying extra on your mortgage, you are doing so

  into a redraw account so that you also have enough savings to cover emergencies.

- If all your assets are in retirement funds, leave them there. Chances are they are getting higher interest than your mortgage is costing you, and you are often penalised for withdrawing them anyway.

- Co-contribution. While you're still in the work force, take advantage of employer and government cocontribution schemes that reward you by topping up your super payments when you make deposits. This is essentially 'free' money and is worth much more in the long run than paying extra on your mortgage.

Whether you pay off your mortgage or not is an individual choice. Things like how long you have left in the work force, what your balance is, whether you can access mortgage interest tax breaks through things like negative gearing, and what savings or investments you have will all come into play.

Talk to your accountant, do your sums, and see what works best for you. The most positive actions you can make at this point are sensible money choices and capitalising on the things you have.

Why a deposit is important

The more deposit you put down, the smaller the loan you will have, and the better your chances of paying it off quicker and saving hundreds of thousands in the process.

If it's a choice between a cheaper home with a bigger deposit or a dearer home with a smaller deposit, the bigger deposit comes out trumps every time.

Why do you have to save a 20% deposit? Well, technically you don't—some banks will let you get away with only a 5% deposit, which on a $500,000 house is only $25,000.

But $25 grand is still a decent whack of moola and can be hard to scrounge when you already feel like you're digging deep.

And don't forget that in some countries, paying less than 20% deposit means you'll need mortgage insurance.

Lenders mortgage insurance (LMI) or higher lending charge (HLC)

What is mortgage insurance? Essentially, dead money. It is money you give the bank in addition to your loan if you don't have a 20% deposit. It makes them feel better about taking on what they see as a 'risky' client and it helps you... not at all. It's charged by the lender if your mortgage has a high loan—deposit ratio and is designed to cover any increased risk they may have by taking you on.

Mortgage insurance is *not* income protection for the borrower; that is a whole other kettle of fish. LMI is exactly what the name suggests: Insurance for the lender—not the borrower. If something bad happens and the bank needs to sell your house to recoup their money; but it sells for less than what they have invested, then the insurance provider covers that gap. This is what LMI is.

Unlike normal insurance that offers a safety net if something goes wrong, mortgage insurance is akin to throwing your money down the nearest drain or setting it on fire.

At least setting it on fire would be fun (I've always wanted to do that)!

Mortgage insurance literally does nothing for you and is a total waste of money, not to mention it gets added to your mortgage amount, increasing your interest payments and the time paying them!

Based on a $750,000 loan, adding $26,700 in mortgage insurance onto your loan for having only 10% deposit will mean an extra $30,929 paid in interest over the life of your loan. $57,629 smackaroos you literally gave to the bank. I'd be spewing.

You are far better off saving a 20% deposit first than forking out for mortgage insurance.

ORIGINAL LOAN AMOUNT	MORTGAGE INSURANCE PAYABLE WITH A 10% DEPOSIT	INCREASED MORTGAGE INTEREST	TOTAL COST OF LENDERS MORTGAGE INSURANCE
$150,000	$3,366	$3,900	$7,266
$300,000	$6,810	$7,898	$14,708
$500,000	$14,750	$17,086	$31,836
$750,000	$26,700	$30,929	$57,629
$1,000,000	$35,600	$41,238	$76,838

When we bought, we wanted an extra $20,000 on top of our loan to renovate (we bought the worst house on the street). The bank wouldn't lend it to us without us either increasing our deposit or shelling out for mortgage insurance, both of which made it totally pointless. We ended up just slowly saving for the renovations rather than paying dead money into mortgage insurance.

High-risk loans

Getting a mortgage can be a tricky process for anyone, but if you are self-employed, have a bad credit rating, or no deposit, it can be nightmarish.

Here are some things you can do to help you achieve your loan where others fail, no matter what your 'risk' category.

- Arm yourself with information, know what the banks are going to ask before they ask it, and have the information ready for them. A mortgage broker can help with this.

- Keep track of your spending. If you can show how much (or little) you spend in an average month, the banks will be able to use this to improve your loan standing.

- Save for a larger deposit. The bigger the deposit you have, the less 'risky' you become as a borrower.

- If all else fails and the banks won't give you the time of day, there are always lenders who specialise in 'high-risk' loans. You will probably be up for higher interest rates, but at least you will have your loan. You can always refinance once you've been in the loan long enough for your credit ratings or income to improve. With this in mind, make sure you check out all the exit fees associated with the loan.

- Use online mortgage calculators and play around with figures until you know how much you can borrow, how much you would like to borrow, and how much you need to save to make this a reality. Check out *Chapter 3: 'Make More—Save More'* for help doing this.

- Look at borrowing less. You might not be able to buy the house you want in the suburb you want it. Suck it

  up. You don't have to stay with the same loan or the same house forever. Getting even a small investment property would be better than nothing and will get you started. From little things, big things grow (bloomin jingles always get stuck in my head!).

Self-employed

Getting a mortgage when you're self-employed can be incredibly painful. Even if you're earning great money, banks tend to take a dim view of you because they see you as higher risk. Information is king when you're self-employed, so make sure you know your numbers, your borrowing power, and your future business projections. Here are some ways to combat their preconceptions without going crazy.

- Use an 'online borrowing power' calculator and find out how much you can borrow with what you earn. This will give you a starting point, but be prepared for the bank to say you need to earn more than that as a self-employed person.

- Have your tax returns done and signed off by a chartered accountant for the last 3 years. This is what they base your income assessment on. Unfortunately, that means you can't get a mortgage based on what you are making now, like most people, but on what your average was over those 3 years.

- One of the more common problems for the selfemployed person is their ability to reduce their taxable income with costs most people couldn't claim. While this is great for lowering the amount of tax you pay, it also lowers your taxable income—sometimes leaving you with a figure no one will give you a loan for.

- Ask yourself if it is better to save money by not paying as much tax, or have the ability to get a mortgage. Obviously this would only matter in the run up to getting a mortgage. Once the bank has taken you on, you can go back to claiming as much as possible in tax deductions.

- Put your business on hold and get back in the office, at least until you are settled with a home loan, and then you can give the 9-5 office job the flick again.

- Be prepared for banks to be even more invasive than normal into your finances, your business, and your everyday life. People have even reported banks Googling their businesses and asking for client information. Too far, people! Too far!

Low income

Before even approaching a bank, do your homework. Use an 'online borrowing power' calculator and find out how much you can borrow with what you earn. This will give you a starting point and help you find an option that is right for you.

For lenders, income is the major factor in approving loan applications and in how much they will lend. Typically, what you earn should be able to cover not only your loan repayments, but also ongoing bills and expenses both in your life and to do with your home.

- Make a joint application. Borrow with a partner, a family member, or a friend. If you are doing this, make sure you protect yourself with the correct legal documents.

- Get your credit rating up and lessen any liabilities you currently have.

- Have a larger deposit. You have a far greater chance of success if a lender can see a good savings record. This helps you prove to them that you're not as 'high risk' as you seem on paper.

- Ring your local council member. Sometimes local councils and governments provide tax breaks or help to buy your first home if you are a low-income earner. It never hurts to ask.

- Look at rent-to-buy. While not around so much anymore, you can still occasionally find 'rent-to-buy' properties, which you live in and rent, while simultaneously paying off the house. You normally end up paying quite a bit more in the long run, but it works when you have no other options, and at least you end up owning a house, unlike traditionally renting.

- Check out *Chapter 3: 'Make More—Save More'* and put as many side hustles into place as possible. The more you increase your income, the better your chances of having your mortgage approved.

Single income

If you're playing the mortgage game alone, it is so much harder. I'm not going to lie. Often bills and rent payments are comparative to those paid by couples, without the added benefit of 2 wages to help you save for and pay off a home loan.

The tips we covered for low-income earners are the same for those with a single income. Use as many as you can.

Going it alone does have some benefits. It is often easier for singles to rent out a room in their home to help cover the mortgage and bills. They also only have to answer to themselves, making budgeting much easier. Do whatever you can to make it work for you. It can happen, and it will, if you want it badly enough.

Low credit rating

What is credit rating? Essentially, a record of your credit history or an estimate on whether you, as a person, will be able to fulfil their financial requirements.

Banks, mobile phone companies, and insurers usually do them to see what kind of risk you pose.

Things like paying credit cards, loans, a mortgage, mobile phones, and utility bills on time and in full all add and subtract from your credit rating.

A person who pays for everything in cash and never gets into debt may have a worse credit rating than someone who has a loan, several credit cards and a phone, but always pays their bills—as nobody can 'see' what they are doing. In this way, credit checks can often be unreliable. Here are some ways to get around them.

- Get a copy of your credit rating and work on improving it where you can, or be able to show prospective lenders where you have improved. If your credit rating is ancient history and you have a proven savings record, can show you have paid bills on time and not run up any debt, then banks will be much happier to ignore your credit rating.

- Take steps to settle any outstanding debts. See *Chapter 4* for help with this.

- Look at getting a loan without your spouse. Obviously this will seriously impact your borrowing power, but,

  if they are the only one with a bad credit rating, then it could work out more favourably.

- Look for lenders who see beyond the numbers and don't use credit scoring.

- Avoid having to take out mortgage insurance. Saving a 20% deposit helps your loan avoid being assessed by a mortgage insurer, giving you a greater chance of it being approved.

- Get some help. There are a number of companies who specialise in cleaning up your credit rating. It is possible to get adverse things removed from your credit score.

- Don't shop around. Do, but do it online or through a mortgage broker. Every time your mortgage application is rejected it adversely affects your credit rating. A mortgage broker may be able to tell you which lenders are more likely to take you on before you actually apply. Like having a lawyer, it is important to tell your broker the truth behind your credit rating so they know how best to address the problems.

Whatever your situation, be assured that there is a solution. Use as many of these tips and tricks as you can to ensure you get on the property ladder and start climbing fast!

Key points:

- Information is king! If you are a 'high-risk client,' make sure you have all your employment and expenses paperwork. The more prepared you are, the better your bank visit will go.

- Even if you've already purchased a property, you can make considerable changes to shorten the life, and cost, of your loan.

- Make an informed decision about whether paying off your mortgage in retirement is the right decision for you, and ask professionals for help where needed.

- A deposit is doubly important for 'high-risk' borrowers; it helps achieve a loan and minimises both loan term and interest payments.

- It is cheaper to save a deposit first than pay mortgage insurance.

Hopefully that's given you some great ideas on how to get what you need from banks, even in tough situations. Next up, we look at finding a good house and a great area, buying in areas you can't afford, and buying new vs. renovating, along with some other burning questions. You'll find all this in *Chapter 8: What and Where to Buy*.

CHAPTER 8
WHAT AND WHERE TO BUY

"When you determine what you want you have made the most important decision of your life. You have to know what you want in order to attain it."—Douglas Lurton

What and where you buy are both determined by what you can afford. Over the last 5 chapters we have looked at budgets, debt, how to cut the fat, and save a deposit. You should now have a fairly good idea of how much you have left at the end of every week.

In *Chapter 5* you worked out your 'magic formula': the amount you could actually afford to spend on a home in order to pay it off in under 10 years.

If you didn't do this, go back and re-visit it, because for this chapter you will need those figures.

What are you looking for?

You know how much you can afford, but do you know what you want? Sometimes we have so many ideas rattling around in our brains about what our home must have and look like that it is hard to differentiate between the 'must have' and the 'wouldn't it be nice.'

Sit down with whomever you're buying a house with and go over exactly what you want in a home. You can print off our My

Home Checklist[24] and use this as a guide, or you can draw up your own. Write down everything you can think of, from picket fences to solar power, garages, decks, and number of rooms.

Once you've got everything down on paper, start organising them into the 'must have,' 'yes please,' and 'added bonus,' sections. Be honest with yourselves. If you know what is written on your check-list is accurate, you won't have to waste time visiting open homes that just don't have what you need, and it makes it super easy to compare individual homes.

When we bought, the things that were important to us were good bones, foundations, and area, and either a large garage or the space to put one in. It took us 2 years to find our home, but we haven't looked back and it is everything we wanted. Stick to your guns and make sure the things that are important to you come first.

Picking an area

When we first moved to Sydney we rented a house in 'The Shire.' The Aussies call it 'God's Country' and 'The Bubble,' and we loved it on sight! When we went to buy, however, we found that the places we were looking at were several *hundred* thousand dollars out of our price range. Not wanting to move out of The Shire, we started having a look at some of the suburbs on the fringes that were within our budget. Most of them we discarded for one reason or another: Too many apartments, too far out, really run down, not a great vibe, and limited public transport.

But one place really stuck out. It was built between two national parks so couldn't be over-developed, it was 20 minutes from

---

[24] http://www.how2without.com/bonus-materials/mortgage-free-workbook/

our favourite beaches, had great schools and all the main shops—supermarkets, banks, cafés, butchers, etc. It also just had a great vibe, there were lots of families and dogs, and people just seemed friendlier.

We ended up buying our house here and have never regretted it. Not long after moving in, they built a massive new playground 5 minutes down the road and updated the community centre and shopping precinct. The house prices have now doubled and it is becoming increasingly hard to even find a house to buy, let alone pay for it.

This is the kind of area you need to look for:

One that ticks all the boxes, but might be that little bit further away, or not as upmarket as you're used to. Chances are, you already have an idea about where you want to buy, but if you don't, or if that place is now out of your price range, have a look at some of these things to consider when picking an area.

- Check the statistics on suburbs in your area and see which ones have increased drastically in price over the last 5 years and which haven't.

- Go and explore areas you haven't visited before and get a 'feel' for the places that haven't yet jumped in price.

- Look at whether there is a reason the house prices are lower. Is it a horrible spot? Is transport an issue? Or has it just not been discovered yet?

- Eliminate the suburbs that are not in your price bracket and focus on the ones with houses that you can afford. Be sure to keep an eye out for mortgagee auctions and deceased estates, as these can often go cheaper than the local price range, and get you into an otherwise unaffordable area.

- Look at the geography of places. Can they be overdeveloped or built out? Are they prone to flooding, bush fires, tornadoes, or earthquakes?

- Do you have to get in your car to access shops and schools, or can you walk?

- Are there local schools and colleges, and are they good ones?

- Is there public transport or good roadways?

- Have some of the surrounding suburbs recently become too expensive?

- Are there any local attractions? Museums, walks, beaches, etc.

- What is the demographic? Are there families? Retired people? Professional couples? Does this fit with what you are looking for?

- Are there any safety issues in the neighbourhood? Gang problems? High crime statistics? A larger than normal police presence that might indicate other underlying problems?

- Is there any local industry that can provide jobs, or would you have to travel? Is it a stable, long-term industry, unlike mining and forestry, which are short term?

- Are the land lots a comparative size to surrounding suburbs? One town in NZ allowed developers to subdivide already small sections to build houses and alleviate the housing shortage. It has essentially become a slum, (as much as anywhere in NZ can get, anyway), with low prices attracting the lower socioeconomic bracket instead of a broad cross-section. Its crowded streets have one of the worst crime rates in the vicinity, and the police and the neighbourhood in general have trouble with gangs and drug-related issues.

- Are there good cafés, shops, waterways, parks, and other features that will help to add value to your property?

All of these things are worth considering when you're looking at areas. Don't just go with what you know and what you are comfortable with. Research and then research some more. It could very well pay off in a big way.

Domain in Australia has a fantastic new property price guide[25] that allows you to view the street view of a home and how much its estimated worth is, both to buy and to rent. This could be invaluable if you are comparing several areas, or if you are looking at purchasing in an area you do not know.

It doesn't claim to be 100% accurate, but it gives you a fair idea of prices and rental yield based on homes in the area, recent sales, and any other relevant data they can get their hands on. Tools like this can save a lot of time when you're researching areas, and provide just as much, if not more, correct information than many other sources.

When good areas go bad

Occasionally areas that were once gems in their time begin a slow but fatal decline and eventually become areas no one wants to live in, let alone buy a property in. Sometimes this is due to work leaving an area. No industry = no jobs. Sometimes areas become cut off due to transport issues or natural

---

[25] http://www.domain.com.au/property-profile

disasters. Occasionally it is simply the presence of too many undesirable factors that drives an area down.

Whatever the reason, there are almost always telltale signs. Large companies generally know they have a limited run left (although I will never forget Ansett Airlines' overnight closure), and if you make enquires or consult the mighty Google you can find out a lot about an area. Look at council websites and see what development work is on the cards, and drive around town and see how house-proud the neighbourhood is. I find this tells you a lot.

Drive around in the daytime and the nighttime. How safe do you feel? What comes out at night that you didn't see in the day? Would you be happy to walk or take public transport in the evenings? What are people doing during the day? Are there families around? How many people are in the cafés?

Be cautious, but be realistic. Not everyone keeps their lawns mowed as often as they should. Guilty! Some areas perk back up after having an injection of jobs from tourism or new work sources, too. Just do your best to weed the good from the bad and make sure you don't buy in an area just because it is cheap.

'Can't afford' the area you love?

Love, love, love a particular area but there's no way you can afford it? This may happen. Don't give up, however; there are ways around this, and just because the area you love is out of reach doesn't mean every great area is! Broaden your horizons and see if you can find something further afield. You may be pleasantly surprised.

- Are you looking at the best house in the area? Stop looking at the end game and start looking at a level you can actually afford. You might not be able to start off with the house of your dreams, but you can definitely work your way there over time!

- Buy a property with a friend or family member. A friend of mine bought an apartment with her brother when she was just 20. She and her husband now own 3 homes, and her original apartment in a beach suburb has appreciated nicely over the years. Just make sure you protect yourself and do everything through a lawyer, so if something goes bad you're covered. My friend and her brother had separate mortgages that they could pay off at whatever speed suited them.

- Remember that nothing is forever. You may start off buying in a neighbourhood you're not enamoured with, but that doesn't mean you have to stay there! Pay off some or all of your loan and you will then be in a far better position to buy in the suburb you want to live in.

- Think about buying an investment property instead of a home and renting a place for yourself that suits you more. You need to make sure that the rent from your home covers either your mortgage or your outgoing rent, though, and consider other drawbacks, like having to move if the landlord requires it or rent prices going up.

- Buy in another state or country. There are many drawbacks to doing this, including having to hire property managers, not being present if difficulties arise, having to travel to see houses or rely on property agents to pick them for you, and of course, not knowing the area as well or at all. The advantages, however, can be many and varied. You are able to buy a cheaper house, put renters in it, and pay it off fast! Especially if you aren't paying rent yourself.

- Take up Couch Surfing[26] or live with the 'olds.' Flat with friends or rent a small studio or granny flat. All these options can help you save enough money to buy a house and put renters in it. Use the rental return and the money you save living on the cheap to pay off your mortgage. Not many people still want to be living at home in their 30's and up, but if it helps you get ahead, it might be worth the hardships.

- Split homes. Look for homes that could be easily separated into two dwellings or have already been kitted out as 'extended family living' or 'home and income' packages. Another friend of mine bought her home with her parents. It is a 2-story home with a lovely yard and pool, which they share. There is internal access to the top level where her parents live, but the two levels are totally separate in the sense that they each have their own bathrooms, kitchens, and bedrooms. They will often go for days without even bumping into each other. Some places have separate access, too, which is great if you are not sharing with family.

- Granny flats can also be a great money spinner, and it can be worth paying a bit extra for a home with a granny flat already in place. For example, a home comes up for $500,000 with a self-contained granny flat already in place. Your repayments for a 10-year mortgage would be $1,387 a week.

  However—your tenants would be covering some of that expense. Assuming the granny flat were to rent for $300 a week, your weekly repayments would be $1,087. You could even rent out the main home for around $800 a

---

[26] http://www.couchsurfing.com

week and live in the granny flat. This would then only leave you $587 a week to pay on your mortgage.

GRANNY FLAT SAVINGS

- Weekly payments
- Granny flat income
- Adjusted payment

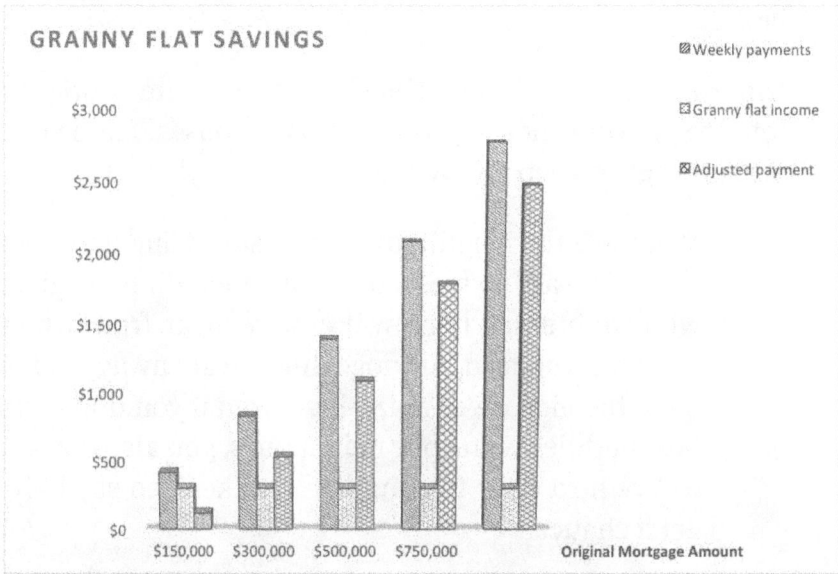

And this is based on a home worth half a million! You can certainly find cheaper homes than that, getting your mortgage repayments so low that the rent you make might even pay for the mortgage. Heaven.

How to choose a house

You should now know the areas you want to buy in, how much you can afford—actually—and what sort of things to look for in a potential property.

Once you start going to open homes, the real fun begins (cue sarcasm). We went to open homes almost every weekend for 2 years, and while initially fun, we were so over it by the time we bought. I still see the realtor signs for open homes and shudder—ever so thankful that side of it is done and dusted!

Whenever you attend an open home, take a checklist with you. You always think you will remember specific things about each place, but believe me when I say they all blur into one after a while.

Print off our Open Homes' Checklist[27] and write yourself some notes to jog your memory and compare houses. Here are some of the things to keep an eye out for.

- If you see the neighbours, try to say hi and get a feel for them. We are so blessed to have incredible neighbours who we literally borrow a cup of sugar from when we need to, who feed our dog while we are away, and drive us to the airport. A-maze-ing! Even if you don't end up best buddies with your neighbours, you also don't want to live next door to complete plonkers, so say hi if you get a chance.

- What could you immediately do to make the property more valuable? Think outside the square. Not every property has curb appeal, but most can. Look over the best renos list in *Chapter 9* and have a good look round. If you want to use your homes equity to invest, then this can be an easy first step.

- Check that any extensions or renovations have been done legally and well. Nothing devalues a property quicker than bad renovations. And if neighbours complain to the council about the new front room that blocks their sun, you may find yourself living in a 3bed place instead of the 4-bedroom one you paid for.

- Assess the neighbourhood. See what's in the local area—parks, schools, churches, waterways. Ask the

---

[27] http://www.how2without.com/bonus-materials/mortgage-free-workbook/

realtor if he can recommend a café and go for a coffee. Sometimes it's the best way to get a feel for a community. You'll also probably need one after viewing 5 homes!

- Ask if there have been any recent building and pest inspections performed and if anything was found. Eyeball the roof, fencing, cladding, and the internal fixtures, etc., to get an idea of what work on the property would need doing immediately, and also what work would need doing long term.

- How is the access? Can you get a car/boat/camper down the driveway? Is there a busy road that you would need to cross? Are there any right-of-ways or shared access with neighbours?

- Are there any covenants on the property? You can usually see these on the original plans. The realtor will often have a copy; otherwise they can be accessed at the local council or lands agency. Often, sewer lines and phone lines will be shared by several properties and companies need access to these. This can mean the garage you wanted to build can't be done and a 'perfect' house becomes a pain in the butt.

- Is the property in a fire/flood/earthquake area? What provisions have been made to protect the property? Would insurance or upkeep cost more because of this?

- If buying an apartment, what are the strata fees and what do they cover? What rules are in place regarding parking, access, noise, washing, etc.?

- Keep an eye out for jobs that are already done. An already-renovated kitchen or bathroom could save you oodles in the long run, and you will often pay less by buying someone else's work than by doing your own, as you generally don't re-coup your money in your selling price. Some other big ones are flooring, roofs, and landscaping.

- What is the age of the house? Does it have insulation or double-glazing on the windows?

- How much maintenance is required both in the short term and ongoing? A ¼ acre section may seem great now, but can you keep it up?

Make sure you bring with you a list of what you're looking for in a property with your price limit written in red across the top. It is so easy to fall in love with a property and to realise too late that not only was it more than you could afford, but it didn't actually tick all the boxes either.

Houses vs. Apartments

Apartments are cheaper to buy and so often seem like the obvious choice to those trying to get onto the property ladder, but that can be an oxymoron.

In Australia, apartments have strata fees—essentially a levy you pay monthly or quarterly. They are normally split into 3 different areas—A 'sink fund' for big things like replacing roofs, an administrative levy for day-to-day things such as gardening and building maintenance, and a special levy for expenses that have no funds allocated to them.

In England, common-hold fees are similar, and in the U.S., coops and condominiums have maintenance fees. These can get really pricey and can range anywhere from a few hundred dollars to many thousands.

In Sydney in 2014, a $4 million apartment in the city was asking for strata fees of almost $10,000 a quarter[28]!!

Make sure you add any associated fees into your calculations. Even if you are saving more in the beginning, you may be paying extra each month.

Statistically, houses also appreciate at a greater rate than apartments, making you more money over the long term than a high-rise. Short term, the appreciation rates are not too different, with apartment prices closing what was once a much wider gap.

In some cities, buying a house is not an option, as land is at a premium. It's not all bad for apartment owners, though. There are no lawns to mow or fences to paint. You are usually closer to work and shops, and some apartments have sought-after facilities such as pools, gyms, 24-hour security, and a concierge service.

New apartment buildings are being built with families in mind, as there is a bigger trend towards city living, and some are even 'green' buildings, utilising solar power and air currents for heating and cooling.

Just make sure you do your homework and ask the tough questions, such as "how much money is in the sink fund" (people have been caught short before, paying thousands for a new roof soon after moving in as the sink fund had run dry), "what facilities are included in the fees" (some co-ops in the States include hot water and rates), "are there rules regarding subletting," and any other things that are important to you, such as hanging washing on balconies and noise restraints.

---

[28] www.domain.com.au/news/youre-paying-how-much-instrata-levies-20141114-11m5vf

Homes that can also have similar issues to apartments are cross-lease sections, semi-detached homes, gated communities, and terraces. Check before purchasing, as things such as shared driveways, walls, and security measures mean you are now answerable to other people for things that owners of standalone dwellings don't have to worry about.

Houses have none of these fees or restraints attached. It is more your own to do with as you like. You can sublet, run on the treadmill at 5 a.m., and let your dogs and kids run wild in the backyard, all without huge fees. Of course, you have to pay for your own roof to get replaced and mow your lawns, but I think it's worth it. Whether you choose an apartment or a house really depends on what is important to you. Just make sure you take all the related expenses into account.

Buying new or renovating

Buying a new house has its pros and cons.

Firstly, you don't have to do any work. Awesome. You can just move in and get on with paying off your mortgage. However, this will often mean you pay substantially more for the property in the first place.

If you are not handy or your time is worth more working at your job than renovating, then buying new might be a good option. Look out for any perks such as new home tax rebates, and also any costs such as the 'extras' that a lot of companies don't include if building a new home, such as buying curtains, carpet, and fixtures.

Buying a renovated house can be tricky. Some renovated houses are great. They have had wiring and plumbing replaced, kitchens and bathrooms renovated, and paint, plaster, carpets, and fixtures revamped. Often the owner cannot market the house for enough to cover their costs, so you get a 'new' house without the price tag.

Often though, a house has just received what I call a 'Dulux overhaul' (Dulux is a paint brand in Australia). This is a house that has only been renovated superficially to make it more marketable. You are often paying a fully renovated price tag without the costly work actually being done. Don't touch these if you can help it. Not only are you paying more, but you will also still have to invest time and money doing the hard work they should have done. Any profits you make will be nonexistent because you already 'paid' for them in the purchase price.

Buying a dump has its own craziness attached. This is what we did. We literally bought the worst house on the street. However, with my father-in-law in the building trade, my dad a sparky, and my hubby an engineer who grew up on building sites, we had more than a fair idea on how to do most things ourselves.

The other benefit of buying what many see as a dump (including myself on rough days), is that you will get it for a lot less, be able to renovate it however you want, and you can do it in your own time frame as money allows. This isn't always fun. I see my pink hallway and green bathroom some days and wish we had done things differently. Then I look at my bank account and am so glad we didn't!

The most important aspect of any house is to ensure that the bones are good—that it is structurally sound and will be around for many more years to come. Get a building and pest inspection done and make sure you know if there are, or have been, termites, rot, sagging foundations, roof leaks, or things like asbestos, easements, or right-of-ways. Also check what the land used to be. New developments built on swamps, sand, and reclaimed land may look great now, but can often lead to massive problems later on. If you start with good bones, you can change the body however you like.

Some other things to note are:

- Generally speaking, never buy at the bottom or at the top of the market in your chosen area—look for something in the middle for the best deals. We bought at the bottom of the market, but it just takes a bit more knowledge. If you think you're up for it, then by all means, do.

- Buy somewhere you will be happy to stay for at least 10 years. The more you move the more money you will bleed.

- Look at how you could further develop the property in the future. Is there room for a garage, a granny flat, or even another house? Could you add a second story or another room?

- Never, ever buy a house without viewing it. When we were looking at homes to buy, my husband and I found what looked like a lovely cottage on a decent section within our price range. When we viewed it, however, there was so much damp and decay there were actually maggots crawling over the ceiling. We couldn't get out fast enough.

  Real estate agents are very clever at taking photos that only show off the good traits in a home and none of the bad. Why wouldn't they? The more people who view it, the greater their chance of a sale. Always make sure either you or someone you trust sees the property in person, as well as getting an inspection done.

Don't be fooled by their terminology, either. Cosy does not mean comfy, it means small!

Key points:

- Work out what you want in a home, before you start looking.

- Buying in great areas is not always impossible on a budget.

- Choosing a great area is even more important than a great house.

- Do your research and study any potential areas, cities, and countries.

- Consider ALL the costs involved when choosing between homes and apartments.

Whatever house and area you choose, make sure it fits you and any changes to your life you envisage happening in the next 10 years.

Once you've got that nailed, look at the *Steps to Your Home* in *Chapter 9*. It includes information on costs, real estate agents, the sale process and renovations and their impact on your property value. Jump in and take a look!

CHAPTER 9
STEPS TO YOUR HOME

"If you haven't found it yet, keep looking. Don't settle. As with all matters of the heart, you'll know when you find it."—Steve Jobs

Costs of buying

Make sure you have a handle on all the costs associated with buying a property—stamp duty, building and pest inspections, lawyers' fees, conveyancing fees, bank fees, council fees for accessing records or renovating, insurances for building and content, or landlord insurance. These will be different everywhere, but can add up fast.

Dealing with real estate agents

This was our most hated part of the whole home-buying process. Realtors tend to be pushy and are often rude and overbearing. They almost always want your contact details when you attend an open home, and you are then left to fend off calls and emails asking what you thought, or offering you similar homes.

It didn't seem to matter how many times we told them what we were looking for or what our price range was, they would always ring with 'the perfect house' that didn't even come close to what we wanted, and was nowhere within our price range. It was hard not to go raving mad!

- Try to only give out one set of contact details and put realtor numbers in your phone if you can. This allows you to ignore calls from overly annoying agents if you are at work or otherwise engaged.

- Be firm with them. Remind them (continuously) of what you are looking for and in what price range. Ask them not to call with homes outside these specifications.

- Encourage them to show you all the homes on their books that have the right specs, in one go, so you don't have to wait for open homes. This can help you get in first with offers, and it means you can then attend the open home to look for a second time.

- Make sure you have a very clear line of communication between yourselves, the realtor, and the owner. Our real estate agent was hopeless, and even though we had agreed on a six-week settlement, harassed us every other day over our final payment, and in turn made the owner so anxious we 'weren't going to come up with the money' that we almost lost the property.

- Remember that they have their own best interests at heart, not yours, and not the owners'. The more money they can get out of you, the higher their commission. If they say there is another bidder, take it with a grain of salt. There may be, but then again he could be imaginary.

- When all's said and done, though, there are some absolutely lovely agents who will go out of their way to help you, who ring with awesome houses, and who are a fount of useful information—(don't buy that one, it floods, and that one has rising damp). I truly hope you get one of these wonderful people on your side and that house hunting is a breeze!

Auctions vs. Private treaty

How is the home being sold? There are many different ways for properties to go under the hammer. Auctions are one, mortgagee sales are another. Private treaty is the most common, and some are advertised under POA or 'price on request.' However the home you want is listed, remember your budget and be smart.

I hate auctions, and find that most of the houses go for more than what I want to pay, as people go crazy in the heat of the moment. Often, though, there is no choice unless the owner will accept an offer before going to auction.

If you do end up with 50 other people at an auction, try not to get caught up in the hype. There will be a lot happening—noise, the auctioneer rabbiting on, realtors and lenders coming over trying to get you to up a bid or feel out where you're at, and of course bidding.

Remember you have a limit! Write it down and stick to it. Take someone with you who will drag you away once that limit is reached. I know, I know, it's only 2 grand more... but that 2 grand quickly becomes 10 or 20 or 50, and soon your budget is totally blown.

Don't be bummed if it only sells for 5 grand over your limit. If you had bid that extra 5 grand, chances are the winning bidder would have bid higher too. It wouldn't have stopped there.

Private treaty—buying houses with an advertised price, is always much easier, I find, although they have their own pitfalls. In an auction, at least you know who you're competing against and that they are genuine. In a private sale, not only are your opponents faceless, but you also sometimes wonder if they exist at all. Never offer the asking price straight up. Offer less. The real estate agent will generally either tell you straight up that there is no way the owners would accept that, or that he will put the offer to them. Sometimes they will even say that it is below a current offer. So, then begins the backwards and forwards between the owner, the realtor, yourself, and any other interested parties. If you're lucky, you'll be the last man standing with a good offer in place.

POA houses are often sold as such for two reasons. The first is to garner curiosity from the public on what the house will sell for. You end up looking more closely at the pictures trying to gauge the price line and can even become 'hooked' on a property without even knowing the price. The second is to net a wider range of individuals who may not have looked at the house if it had an advertised price of more than they could afford. Once you have made an enquiry, they can keep your details and call you with other homes or push the worth of the original property.

Mortgagee auctions are like normal auctions, only they have the ability to go for a lot less–or not. The lenders only want a property to sell for how much they are owed, and there is no 'passing in' of a property if it doesn't gain the heights its owners want. The bank wants that house sold and its money back. Mortgagee sales can be great for getting a house cheap enough for some serious mortgage repayments to happen.

How much do you offer?

When we were buying our first home, we ended up paying more than we wanted. We had placed several bids along with three other interested parties, and finally, our last competitor dropped off. The house was almost ours. The owner, however, didn't want to let it go 'so cheaply.'

It was so frustrating! There was no one else bidding. What were we supposed to do? Bid against ourselves? Then my husband remembered the advice he'd been given by a friend who had seen several properties lost for want of stubbornness and a few grand. "Don't quibble over a couple of thousand dollars."

Now I know I keep telling you to stick to your budget, but there is of course a flip side to the coin. We knew our property was a good one. It was structurally sound, it checked all our boxes, it was in a great area, and was the worst house on the street. We sucked it up and asked the owner how much their sell price was. It was $3,000 more than our last offer.

Should he just have taken our offer? Probably, because sellers have also lost many buyers by quibbling over small amounts. But that was his sell price, and 3 grand in the scheme of things was a drop in the bucket. We paid the extra. We still felt like we got a good house for a good price, and you know what? It's now worth twice what we paid for it.

Just because an owner is being stubborn or someone else has bid more, doesn't always mean you should, though. Bidding wars can often get out of control and you end up a lot more over budget than 3 grand. Always refer back to your limit and make sure you account for any upfront costs such as immediate work that needs doing, and buying costs.

A dearer house with no renovations to make may actually be 'cheaper' in the long run than a less expensive home that needs a lot of work. And remember, it's not over till the fat lady sings.

I have heard countless stories of people 'missing out' on houses, only to get them later on when a sale falls through.

Losing the 'perfect' home

Just because you've found the home you want to buy doesn't mean you'll get it. It can often be a competitive market, especially for homes in the lower price ranges. Here are some tips to get you through the chaos.

Try to remember it is not the only house for sale! We missed out on 3 places before we finally got our first home. We were outbid on all of them. Every occasion it happened I was a bit bummed. That was 'the one!' But each time, another house eventually popped up that was just as good, and the house we eventually bought was better in many ways. Don't let your vision of the perfect house blind you to the fact that there are many more and force you into paying more than you should.

Try not to become fixated on a home. Keep going to open homes even while you are placing an offer on another. If it falls through, hopefully you will already be looking at some other lovely properties.

Cooling off period

Some sales (normally only private treaty, not auction) can be negotiated with a cooling-off period. This normally starts the day you and the owner sign the contract and lasts anywhere from 24 hours to a week. It is essentially a breathing space where you calm down, check everything with the bank, and check last-minute things before finalising the sale.

If you cancel the sale in this time frame, though, there is almost always a cost; sometimes a quite hefty one, as it's normally based on a percentage of the sale price. Make sure you have all your i's dotted and t's crossed beforehand to avoid any problems.

You can waive your right to a cooling off period, and if you're sure everything is okay, then this can be a good idea to speed up the process.

The interminable wait

Yay! Your offer has been accepted, the cooling off period is over, and now you have to get all your ducks in a row.

You will exchange contracts with the owner.

Once your conveyancer or solicitor has looked the contract over, you will sign it and you will be asked to put down a 10% deposit.

That horrendously large cheque is still to date the most terrifying one I've ever written. There's no going back once that's handed over!

A settlement date will be arranged where you will have to provide the remaining monies.

Get yourself to the bank ASAP and get your mortgage sorted out. Unless you haven't listened to anything I said, you should have a pre-approval with your bank already, and they will now only need to re-check paperwork and formally approve it before setting it up. Be ready to jump a few more hurdles before the mortgage account is finally up and running, and double check everything! You don't want to be finding out you have no redraw and you have a massive exit fee after the paperwork is all signed.

Once everything is complete you just have to wait the agreedupon time. This is normally between 4 and 8 weeks, but can be negotiated with the owner. Some don't mind a shorter wait, while others may find a longer settlement date works better, especially if they are selling another home or moving from far afield.

Make sure the owner is following through on any agreements, such as rubbish removal and clearing out the house.

Your title deeds and mortgages will be registered once the mortgage is complete, and you then get the keys to your new home!

Make sure you get a photo in front of the sold sign for your photo album!

Getting the keys

The day we got our keys was up there with the most exciting days of my life. We ripped up old carpets and threw blinds and rotten cupboards out the back door in under an hour. There were so many visions of change and so many expectations wrapped up in those walls, it was hard to think about one thing too long without another one popping up.

If you're planning on doing big renovations, take photos of all the rooms so you can see how much things have changed in the years to come.

We invited friends out to dinner to celebrate, and I just couldn't get the smile off my face. It was so exciting. We actually owned a house. Well, the bank did. We probably owned the front porch.

But that night the mortgage was the last thing on my mind. The excitement filled up all the space where doubt usually lurks and I was just super excited. Enjoy it! You have taken the first step in one of life's biggest fields.

You have a house!

That excitement is going to tide you over the settlement period and hopefully a fair way into your first year. Before you can pick up the keys, though, there are a few things you need to do.

- Give your current landlord (if you have one), notice. You normally only have to give 4 weeks, so you should only have to do this once your purchase is in place, but just check your lease to be sure.

- Get yourself some insurance for at least your building, if not the contents as well. Building insurance is nonnegotiable and will be required by the bank. You can either use the bank's favoured insurer or pick your own. Make sure to compare prices and find out which suits you the best.

- There are quite a few online calculators that make it easy to compare insurers. Make sure that you choose one that will pay for the total re-building cost or that you can set a high figure to rebuild. Many people have been caught out having to pay the gap between what their home was insured for and what it actually cost to rebuild.

- Connecting your power, water, and landline. Again, shop around. Don't just assume that the company your folks have always used is the best. Look! Companies often offer great deals and sign-up specials to new customers. You are usually up for a connection fee, but some companies will even waive this.

- Cleaning and initial overhaul. Start thinking about what needs doing to the house, how much of that needs to be done before moving in, and how much can wait until you can afford it. When we bought our home it was filthy! An elderly gentleman had lived there before us, and his eyesight and health had been failing.

Before we could move in, we tore out all the rotting carpet and curtains, completely stripped the kitchen of all shelving, benches, and oven. (There were so many years' of ingrained grime we couldn't even salvage them.) And we cleaned. Everything.

Our neighbours from our old property came over (God love them!), and we scrubbed walls, ceilings, floors, and everything in between. They were literally running black as we scrubbed. We also painted our room white, as I didn't think I could wake up to lime green every day, and we replaced the toilet seat. It cost us about a week of rent and $100 in paint and cleaning products—then we moved in.

Hopefully your clean won't be as drastic as ours, but you might have broken window glass or new locks to install or rubbish to get rid of. These really should be done before you move in. Things like re-painting walls and polishing floor boards are certainly easier if you are not already living in a home, but just remember that it is not only the cost of doing these things that add up, but also your rental expenses for the weeks you do it. You can always put all your furniture and belongings into a couple of rooms, paint and clean the rest of the house, and then swap to do the remaining rooms.

- Moving costs. These are many and varied and depend on how far you're moving, how much you're moving, and if there are stairs or difficulties in either of the properties you are moving from, and to. While doing

it all yourself or roping in friends and family may be the cheapest option if you have a small amount of things or a short distance to go, for large trips it may actually be cheaper to hire a truck or a moving company.

10 trips with your car might get everything there, but not only could you damage your vehicle, you will probably pay just as much in gas as 1 trip in a removal truck. I've moved every way possible, I think, and while getting a moving company to do everything for you is by far the easiest way, it can be very expensive. Pack yourself (ask supermarkets or appliance shops for boxes), and then consider renting a truck for a day. You can normally fit everything in one trip, and then you only have to worry about unpacking at the other end.

- International travel or travel to other states is trickier. Make sure you're not paying more to move furniture than it is worth. It might be cheaper to sell it and buy it again at the other end. Consider having a yard sale and selling off all the things you never use so that you pay less in freight. Sell enough and it may even pay for your move!

Renovations and your property value

High cost and time renovations like knocking out walls and updating kitchens and bathrooms, leave be. Not only are they money pits, but you can live without them. Yeah, it sucks to use old stuff, but it doesn't kill you. If you've got an extra $20,000 to do large renos it would be better spent adding it to the mortgage.

Don't get me wrong, I think renovations are a great way of keeping from going insane while paying off your home; they add a sense of achievement and slowly making your home brighter helps you stick at it. However, they don't all need to be done at once, or even straight away. When you do renovate, look at which things make the biggest difference to your life and increase the property's value.

When renovating, keep an eye to the future, and if you are not planning to retire in your new home, make sure the renovations are tasteful and cater to the many, not the few, so that when you go to sell, you will get more interest and ultimately more money.

That means no purple flocked walls or bright pink tiles. Get a few friends to come through and point out all the things they don't like, or would immediately see or question when coming to an open home. Fix as many of these things as possible. You'll find some of them are really simple, such as changing a light shade or a door handle.

10 best renovations

Do you want to create a more usable space or make sure your home brings top dollar when you sell? Check out the most sought after renos that will tick all the boxes without blowing your budget.

1. Create space and flow by knocking out non-structural walls and removing things like kitchen islands and shelving that block movement and views.

2. Landscaping—one of the top 3 things you can do to increase a property's value can be as simple as weeding a garden. Adding a new garden, path, or fence can also add tremendous curbside appeal to a house and really up your profit margin.

3. People often judge a house by the first 7 seconds of viewing. Make sure your approach, entrance door, and the room you're entering into are all up to scratch.

4. Refurbish the bathroom without completely renovating it. Replace the toilet seat, change old handles for new, replace the taps and faucet, clean grout, paint over garish tiles, repair anything that is broken or leaky, add a shelf, a plant, and swap out the frosted glass for clear. All these things add a breath of fresh air without the price tag.

5. Give the inside and the outside a new coat of paint where needed. Use neutral tones that will suit the majority of people and add your colours with removable things such as throws, pillows, and home wares.

6. Update your kitchen. Paint it, add some new tiles or glass splash-backs, or simply change the cupboard doors or door handles. Even changing little things in the kitchen can make a big difference. For example: If you have a really old extraction fan, pull it out. Get a new one if you can afford to, but personally I would rather have none than a 50-year-old, clunky fan covered in other people's grease.

7. Check out the flooring. People often see floors as a big expense even if they're not. Fix squeaky floorboards, rip up stained carpet and either re-carpet, or if you have nice floorboards, sand them back and varnish. Look at getting floating floorboards to cover a concrete slab. Even laying vinyl can be an improvement. If you live in a more modern place, getting your concrete slab polished can be a cheaper alternative to adding floor coverings, and looks really cool.

8. Re-invent a space. Finish that attic or basement room, create a living space with sofas and a wet weather rug

on your deck, or transform your garage into an extra room or office.

9. Build a deck. Outdoor space is highly regarded whether you have a big yard or a little courtyard. There are heaps of awesome ideas on how to best utilise your outdoor area—make use of them and live your life more outdoors.

10. Add colour and flair with simple and appropriate décor such as lamps, cushions, artwork, vases and flowers, candles, and throws. Make sure your decor suits the era and style of your house. Not only does it look weird having modern homewares in a simple cottage, or rustic pieces in a modern mansion, it will detract from the home and diminish your selling price.

10 worst renovations

Some renovations are nice, but just not worth the money unless you are planning never to sell. Think long and hard before investing in any of these and ask yourself why you want to do them. If it is because you really want to and plan on spending the next 20 years in this home, then by all means go for it. But if you are doing it to increase your property value, be warned, you will not make it back.

1. Installing a pool. Not only is this incredibly expensive in the short term, with fencing, planning approval, and the actual development costs, it can also be costly over time with chemicals, water, and upkeep. Not everyone views a home with a pool as a good thing, and it may actually stop people from buying a property.

2. Adding a home office. While the thought of working from home might sound great, spending money on an office will give you far less return than just leaving it

   as a room. Not only are people looking for space, those who would like an office are usually just as happy doing it themselves. Let's face it; offices just aren't exciting.

3. Sunroom addition. Not only are you paying to add to the footprint of a house, you are adding massive windows and you can only use the room for relaxing. You can't put your guests in there, or they would wake up with the birds every morning, and unless you live in Alaska, it is often too hot for a large portion of the year. If you really have a desire to add to your home, adding a bedroom will see a greater return than a sunroom.

4. Oversized garages. One of the first things we actually did was add a massive garage to our property, but we plan on staying in our home for a long time. We bought a tiny home and garaging is something that is important to us. It is not for everyone, though. While people appreciate the extra storage and the ability to get their car out of the weather, many people just don't see it as important and will pay the same amount for a house without a garage as a house with one.

5. Gourmet kitchens. While a kitchen upgrade is a top reno, going gourmet will totally tank your budget. Not everyone wants a 90-litre oven, designer taps, and marble bench-tops, especially in older or smaller homes. They look out of place, can be seen as pretentious, and your money would be better spent elsewhere.

6. Adding another bathroom. If you can squeeze another bathroom into an existing space, then you might recoup your money. But if you are creating an addition to your house, then odds are you'll never see your money again. While people love the idea of having a second bathroom (especially en suites) they are not prepared to pay $30,000 more for a home to get one.

7. Adding a family room. Adding a big room as a family or entertainment space might be great at relieving stress, but could hit you where it hurts when it comes to selling. Style at Home[29] reckons you would only recoup 50%-75% of a family room reno. Not only are they an unnecessary space, but people often forget to be sympathetic to the outside look of the building when adding on.

8. Doing an 'upscale' roofing upgrade. Roofs are a big expense, and while I suggest looking for a property that has one in good nick, you don't have to spend tens of thousands on new tiles, guttering, and eaves. Just make sure it doesn't leak and looks fresh from the street.

9. Adding a backup power generator. This is not something I have ever thought of, but then, I don't live anywhere that has wild storms or electricity shortages frequently. When our power does go out, it is almost always back on within 24 hrs. If you live somewhere far from civilisation, in an extreme environment, or where there are often power outages, you may get your money back as people will see this as a drawcard. Anywhere else—don't bother.

---

29 http://www.styleathome.com/homes/renovating/ret urn-on-renovation-costs-how-much-will-you-getback/a/882/2

10. Doing a poor job. While DIY may be cheaper, doing things yourself or hiring dodgy tradesman on the cheap could undermine all your hard work. No matter how good an upgrade you put in place, if the workmanship is poor, people will see it straight away and wonder what else is wrong, devaluing your home in a heartbeat. Make sure you don't bite off more than

you can chew and carefully vett all tradies via word of mouth or a guarantee.

Key points:

- Know what you want in a home, and take your checklist with you to open homes.

- Only give out one set of contact details to realtors, and have a clear line of communication with them.

- Know how much you can offer, and make sure to include buying costs and the cost of immediate repairs and renovations.

- Make sure all your ducks are in a row so there are no problems when finalising your mortgage.

- Ensure you give notice, sort your move, and finalize details with the seller before picking up keys.

- Check the top and bottom 10 renovations, and make sure you're capitalizing on your property.

Getting to this point has been a whole lot of craziness and hard work. Up next in *Chapter 10*, find out how to *Survive Your Loan Term*. We look at changes in circumstance, dealing with dramas (and people), having support, and your critical first years. But for right now, enjoy. You've done so well!

CHAPTER 10
SURVIVING YOUR LOAN TERM

"Success is not final; failure is not fatal: it is the courage to continue that counts."—Winston Churchill

Taking that first step over the edge can be so hard. All the work of saving a deposit, finding a house, and dealing with real estate agents is over, and now you have to pay your mortgage every month. It would be so easy to just relax now and pay minimum repayments. If you don't mind having a mortgage till the day you retire. Don't know about you, but no thanks! I've got too many things planned for my life, and they don't involve mortgages and watching my pennies for the rest of my life.

Critical first years

No other time in your mortgage is as critical as the first 3 years. Don't stuff it up!

Anything extra you can pay off your mortgage in these 3 years will make the most difference over the life of your loan. You immediately drop the amount of interest you pay when adding extra payments, and this can double or triple the money you added vs. the money you actually saved. It's pretty awesome.

Be strategic, be careful, and spend smart. Look into all the extra money making ideas from *Chapter 3* and find at least one that suits you. Use that money to either save for holidays and other important things you find you're missing, or to add extra payments to your mortgage. That's extra *extra* payments. You better still be paying double or you will never make your 10year target.

Know one thing for damn sure. The banks and the loan companies do not want you to succeed. They will send letters offering extra credit, reminding you that you can redraw and go on a holiday 'this cold winter,' and ring when you least expect it. If they catch you at a bad time it can be oh-so-tempting.

So if this ever happens to you (or I should say when it happens), I want you to stop and think, "How will this benefit me?" and "How will this benefit the bank?" You can be sure that with thousands of dollars extra in credit card fees or mortgage interest, the banks will be laughing all the way to their... eerm, banks. And you? Well, I am sure you would enjoy the holiday or the new shoes, but are they really worth slogging away for an extra few years and lining someone else's pockets?

Just remember, that as hard as it is, it's not forever. Make yourself a banner and hang it on the wall if you need to. Be proud of what you're doing. Tell your mates (without bragging), and do the happy dance whenever you see that plunging bank balance.

Keeping an eye on the prize—middle years' slog

The excitement, joy, and enthusiasm you started with a few years back may now have waned into a dull acceptance and apathy.

Like 'the little engine who could,' you always seem to be repeating to yourself, "7 more years, 6 more years, 5 more years." Sometimes it seems like the end will never come and that you will be a miser forever.

The middle years I found the hardest. At the beginning it was new and exciting and your clothes didn't look like they had been attacked by a swarm of angry moths. The last few years you had the end in sight and were starting to count down. But the middle few.... sometimes it felt like time had been suspended in a vat of jelly—the yucky flavours—and was crawling along at an infinitesimal pace. Would it ever end? Would there come a time when you didn't add up your restaurant bill before you ordered, or Googled an event to find the cost before accepting a friend's invitation?

Sometimes the only thing that keeps you going is the dream of being debt free and the hope that one day it all would have been worth it.

I found the best way to deal with my 'Eeyore' moments was to log onto my online banking and check out how much we had left on our mortgage and how much was in our redraw account (this shows how much extra you've paid).

This normally cheered me up, and more importantly, helped remind me what I was working towards. I'd text my husband and say things like, "We broke the $200,000-mark last week!!" Or "Only 3 years and 10 months to go." He would always reply with something suitably enthusiastic and I would be over the hump and able to move on.

None of this may be an issue for you! We really pushed our limits paying off our mortgage in 10 years, because we wouldn't budge on the area. This meant that we spent more on our mortgage than I would advise. We knew what we wanted, however, and were prepared to go the hard yards to achieve it.

It just meant money was a little tighter than it hopefully will be for you!

Things you may have to deal with

It wasn't just myself I battled with, though. Everyone seems to have an opinion on your 10-year plan and aren't afraid to share—either their discontent with their 30-year mortgage, their disbelief that 'you live like that,' or your ability to actually achieve mortgage freedom in such a short time frame.

I also battled with peoples' smugness at doing so much more than me. (Okay, maybe I'm reading a bit much into the smugness. Generally, they are just telling me about something with no smugness whatsoever.) It is really hard, though, to see people travelling overseas, eating out, and sleeping under 5 stars when you choose to limit these things, if only temporarily.

Some things you may have trouble with could be:

- Jealousy—it's hard to watch people doing all the 'fun' stuff you can't afford just now. Remind yourself you can afford it—you just choose to pay double mortgage payments. Imagine the fun you can have when your mortgage is gone! Everyone else will be green! Then there's the flip side of the coin—you're not the only one who's jealous. Other people are jealous of you, too! They see you taking a step toward something amazing and wish they had the capacity to do the same. To be able to have a mortgage-free future in sight is incredible. So next time you're feeling jelly, smile, because they are too.

- Self-doubt—it's easy to believe that you just can't do it. After all, isn't that what everyone keeps telling you? YOU CAN ACHIEVE THIS. I did, and you can too. You just have to stick at it. Believe in yourself and find someone else who believes in you too, and who will perk you up when you're feeling down.

- FOMO (fear of missing out)—I have always been like this! Even if I was tired or wanted some alone time, I would still stay up or go out. Who knows what might happen that I could miss out on?! The truth is, you can't be there for everything, and while you may miss out on some things because you just don't have spare cash, the things that you do participate in are that much sweeter because of it. Learn to appreciate the little things and remember how much more you will be able to spend on frivolities in a few short years.

- Disbelief—It's hard for people to accept things that they themselves could not do. If you tell people about your little plan, don't be surprised if you are greeted with disbelief, incredulity, and amusement. In fact, expect it. And be proud. Not everyone can do what you're doing.

- Not enjoying the things you do—Sometimes even when you do get out you just don't enjoy it as much. You always seem to be checking the prices and watching your money, and something you used to love becomes a chore. Stop obsessing about the money! If you've made the decision to go out, then have fun, and make the most of it! Just because you have less in your pocket, doesn't mean you are a different person, just a more considered one.

- Feeling like it will never end—this is especially true of the middle years. But chin up; it's not forever. And even though you can't see it, there is a light at the end of that tunnel. Use whatever tricks you can to remind yourself of your awesomeness. Check your bank account, look at how far you've come, not how far you have left to go, and never lose sight of your goal of being debt free.

- Snide comments—these are what I find the hardest to deal with—I have thin skin! I have had people comment to others in front of me, "Oh, they won't be able to afford that, they're trying to pay off their mortgage in 10 years," or "Do you think you could afford to," or "Are you ordering anything today?" They used to really upset me, but I have learned to just smile or reply with things like, "Sure am! 4 years left" (really pisses them off), or "Nah, I ate before I came, I'm saving up to take my daughter to the snow." Most people don't even know they are doing it (although some do), so don't get too cranky with them. Just breathe and remember that they're still going to be in debt when you're lying on a beach in Tahiti.

- Showing off—be prepared for people to think you are a show-off and are rubbing their noses in their failings too. One of the things I wanted to do when our mortgage was gone was throw a party at our house for all our friends and family who had been with us through our 10-year slog. After a couple of years, though, I realised that the only thing people would see in this was a 'nah nah nah nah,' rather than a thank you. Be careful you aren't that little kid bragging in the playground. Be proud of your achievements, but be modest too. Most people don't want to hear every day that you only have 1 year left on your mortgage, no matter how excited you are!

- The lucky ones—sometimes it seems like your friends have everything. Their Facebook page has pictures of their last holiday in Hawaii, they drive new cars, holidays and nights out are a monthly or even weekly occurrence, and money is like water. But look beneath the surface and you will see that their bank balance is really suffering, they work horrendous hours to make ends meet, and they are worried. Who is really the lucky one here? Count your blessings and enjoy all the day-to-day things that make life awesome. It doesn't have to be expensive to be incredible.

- My personal favourite (please note heavy use of sarcasm) is "You're so lucky!" Seriously!? I'm lucky my husband works his butt off? I'm lucky we go without? I'm lucky we camp instead of hoteling it? WTF, people!!

It doesn't get to me as much anymore, and besides, I heard an awesome quote by Samuel Goldwyn, which I love to reply with, "The harder I work, the luckier I get."

Having a support person on your team

My husband seemed to be impervious to all of this and was always quick to validate our decision, or think of things we could do in lieu of what I was moaning about. We did have lists of things we were going to do with our money once we had our mortgage paid off, and this actually helped keep me on track. Knowing you have guilt-free spending in the foreseeable future is a big draw-card!

I don't think I could have done it without him. Scratch that, I know I couldn't have. Make sure you have a partner, a best friend, or a family member who always has your back. Someone who will remind you of the good stuff when all you see is the bad, and will pull you back on track whenever you stray. Have someone that will hold you accountable for your spending and your saving. They may just be the difference between sticking to your 10-year plan or not.

Extra, Extra repayments

Sometimes you find yourself having a few extra dollars in your pocket more frequently than normal. This might be from a pay rise, a second job, or just because you're getting good at living with less. Take this opportunity to chuck a bit more at your mortgage. While I think it's important to spend some of it and de-stress by taking a holiday, buying some 'stuff,' or eating out for a solid week, if it's more than a one-off influx you could do a lot more.

While the thought of paying yet more onto your mortgage may not fill you with joy, look at it this way. If your circumstances change and you need to redraw on your loan, you could redraw that extra $2,500 you chucked on throughout the year without even altering your 10-year plan. Think of it as back-up money. That rainy-day money is, in the meantime, lowering your interest payments and saving you months on your loan. It's a win-win situation.

Changes in circumstance

Sometimes, against everything you've aimed for and worked towards, things go south. Sometimes slowly, sometimes like a speeding bullet. You might get made redundant, you might have kids, you or a family member might get gravely ill. Whatever the reason, it's crap, but it happens.

Always attempt to solve the problem first. Reducing mortgage payments to make ends meet is only a band-aid to the actual wound. If you do need to reduce payments or redraw, try to give yourself a time limit—'I'll only do it for 3 months,' or look at paying back that money as soon as you're back on your feet.

If you lose your job, try and find work doing anything. $14 stacking shelves or mowing lawns is still $14 more than nothing. Never give up looking, and always believe in yourself. Can you retrain or take advantage of free up-skill courses run by a council? Can you work from home? Ask your friends and former colleagues for introductions. Look outside your job description—plenty of people have found great jobs and even new careers doing things they weren't trained in.

Having kids doesn't mean either giving up work completely or leaving them in daycare. It is just a change. I worked evenings when my daughter was little. We had no family around and I didn't like asking friends on a permanent basis, although we did have some amazing people step up and help us out, for which we will be forever grateful.

Is this something you can do? My husband and I didn't see each other much except on weekends, but it worked until I felt my daughter was old enough for daycare. Can you child share? Look after someone else's kid while they work and vice versa. Can you work longer hours over fewer days? Look at your options and be prepared to juggle!

If you need to move for work, or family reasons, look at renting your home out instead of selling up. You put so much work into choosing a great place. Do your figures and see if you can make it work. It might not be logistically possible, but nothing is forever, and it would be nice to retain something you love even if you're not living in it.

If all else fails and you can't make your payments, don't stress. Whatever you've done so far has already put you further ahead than the average person. That's great! Do what has to be done and use the lessons you've learned to help you in your new battle.

Refinancing and moving

If you've been keeping an eye on your mortgage, you will know how much interest you're paying each month and any other fees the bank is charging. Compare these to similar banks and make sure you're still getting a great rate. A difference of even 1 or 2 percent can make thousands of dollars' difference to your bottom line, and I don't know about you, but I would rather have that money in my pocket than the bank's coffers.

Give the bank a call if you find your interest rate has crept higher than others and see what you can do. If the bank won't play ball, look at refinancing, but remember to do all your sums. The fees associated with setting up a new mortgage may make refinancing a pointless gesture.

Thinking of moving? Get some no-obligation quotes by real estate agents on your property, and then plan accordingly. Time it so you get the maximum amount out of your property. Check capital gains taxes, agent fees, and other costs before you sell, and make sure you will have enough to purchase your new place.

Some banks will let you refinance your original mortgage when selling to buy a new property, but most will make you pay it out and take out another loan. New loan, new fees.

Key points:

- Know what needs doing before moving in and leave the things that can wait till you can afford them.

- When your circumstances change, do your best to continue paying extra on your mortgage or work to repay lapses.

- Don't let other people get you down. Smile and think of Tahiti.

- Always have a support person to help you through the tough times

- The first 3 years are the most critical. Don't mess them up!

Hold fast!

At the end of the rainbow lies a cauldron of gold.

We all know this is a crock, but one thing is for certain. At the end of your road will be financial freedom and a mortgage-free home, years ahead of your peers (kind of works out to a cauldron of gold if you think about it). But you're not there yet!

Keep on keeping on, and never give up. You are the only one who can make this work.

Chapter 11: Life's a Ride, teaches you how to enjoy life during and after your mortgage term, while still sticking to your budget. Find spending, adventure, and holiday tips there.

CHAPTER 11
LIFE'S A RIDE

"Life is short, buy the damn shoes!"—Kenneth Cole

Life's a ride

By now you should have figured out how to have a good time without spending a fortune, and your good habits should have altered your perspective on how much you actually need in life vs. how much of it is just want. There will still be things you struggle with, but look back a few years and see how much things have changed.

Print off our 'Then and Now' worksheet[30] and fill it out. See how far you've come and stay focused!
Every time you have a bad day, drag it out and look at it and congratulate yourself. You really are awesome.

I bet you really enjoy the things you spend your money on now, and get the most out of every purchase and experience.

If none of these things are happening for you, then make sure you are still enjoying life. Just because you're 'broke' (not technically, but you know what I mean) doesn't mean you should let life pass you by! Life is for living, people!

My husband's favourite quote is by Hunter S. Thompson, and it's like it was written for him.

---

[30] http://www.how2without.com/bonus-materials/mortgage-free-workbook/

"Life should not be a journey to the grave with the intention of arriving safely in a pretty and well preserved body, but rather to skid in broadside in a cloud of smoke, thoroughly used up, totally worn out, and loudly proclaiming, "Wow! What a Ride!"

Money, the having or not having, has never stopped him doing anything. He spends time where others do money. His family is the most important thing, and every day of every week he spends time with both my daughter and myself. It might just be sitting together reading, it might be camping, surfing, or exploring together. It might be games on a rainy day (even though he hates them), or the park on a sunny one.

He makes the most out of every minute and never lets the fact that he is married, has a child, and is paying double mortgage payments slow him down. He surfs, rock climbs, and skis when we can afford it, and never complains about 'not having'... whatever

He is my hero.

Be your own hero and make your life count. Write down all the things you enjoy doing on the 'Life's a Ride' worksheet[31] and then find a way to do them. Do the free ones often, the cheap ones occasionally, and save up for the expensive ones so you are always looking forwards instead of backwards.

When it's good to be bad

Sometimes if you don't do something 'bad' you're just going to explode. Kind of like binge eating.

---

[31] http://www.how2without.com/bonus-materials/mortgage-free-workbook/

If you fall off the wagon, don't worry. It's a long road and there are plenty more wagons. Climb back on and keep going. Okay, dodgy metaphor, but really, just because you spent some money or caved on something you regretted (or didn't) later, doesn't mean the world has ended. It just means you're human.

The easiest way to combat this is to give yourself some breathing room and some spending money.

It doesn't have to be a lot. My husband and I got $25 a fortnight each. Sounds like it's not even worth it? Maybe, but it adds up fast, and if we really wanted to buy something we 'couldn't afford,' it was there. I love shoes, new books, and the ability to buy large blue felt hats from the markets. My hubby likes surfboards and skateboards and other outdoors gear—apparently you can never have too much, kinda like shoes.

Our spending money is just for things we want as individuals. If we go out for dinner and the movies we have to come up with that money from elsewhere.

Cut yourself some slack. Make sure you have something every week or fortnight that you can save or spend as you desire. It can make the difference between enjoying life, or being smothered by it.

Going out without going broke

Sometimes I think we live with the belief that no one will like us any more if we don't go out with them every time they ask. Or they won't ask us again. And sometimes this is true—but ask yourself: If someone 'dumps' you because you choose not to go out for lunch every week, how good a friend are they?

Most people (and I know this from experience) will think you are slightly strange or a terrible miser when you say no to the movies/lunch/coffee/paintball, but they don't take it personally. However, you don't always have to say no; there are plenty of options for still enjoying yourself while sticking to your budget.

You can still catch up, just offer alternatives. Coffee? Sure! Come over to my place and I'll make us some. Movies? Yes, I have a two-for-one offer. Lunch? Let's take a picnic down to the river. Sometimes these cheaper alternatives end up being much more fun than the original ideas anyway!

- Take advantage of coupons and special offers. Often you can get some really fabulous deals for up to 80% off. Kids' activities, bowling, eating out, and even special treats like massages. Businesses don't mind when you produce a coupon—they wrote them so you would come to them. Friends also don't mind coupons if it means they get something cheaper! Check the back of your receipts, online deals, and coupon books, and use them when you really want to—not just because it's there.

- You go shopping with a friend and see heaps of things you *really* want. How do you say no? Some of my favourites are: Take note of what it is and add it to a Christmas or birthday list for others to get you. If you try something on and don't absolutely love it in the shop, don't buy it. Find something you love? Leave it in the shop and continue on your merry way. If, at the end of your trip, you are still thinking about what you saw, go back and get it. Before every purchase, think. Do I *need* that or do I *want* it? If it's a want, consider

how much you want it, whether you have the money, and whether you could get it cheaper elsewhere.

If you love going out with your friends on the weekend, it can be an expensive exercise. First there is the taxi in, the entrance money, the drinks and food at the venue, and then the cab home again. Here are some things you can do to make it cheaper.

- Use public transport to get in, or car pool with friends. Eat before you go or take a snack with you so you don't have to purchase food. Drink less and dance more. Not only will your health thank you, you'll have an amazing time and will have spent a fraction of the money.

- Break up your alcohol with water or soft drinks. These are normally free or a fraction of the cost of alcohol, and you'll still have a drink in your hand. Check out places that don't cost to get in or get there before the door fee starts. There are some awesome venues that offer live music and have free entry; many clubs still rely on drinks to make money rather than the door fee.

- If you really want to go somewhere that's expensive, go there and stay there. Don't hop around paying a new fee at each club. If there is no public transport for the way home or it is unsafe late at night, share a cab with a friend to lessen the cost or crash at a mate's till the trains start running again.

Adventures without the bills.

If you like to pack your weekends with fun things to do, or if you're trying to entertain kids over the school holidays, it can be very expensive. There are, though, a plethora of fun things to see and do all around you that are either free or very cheap.

Go for a walk in your local park, swim at the beach or waterhole, meet a friend for a picnic, or have them over for high tea. Get out the board games and the yard games, check online for free events happening in your neighbourhood. Go camping or have a sleepover. Visit a neighbouring town, imagine you are a tourist and visit your own town—we often forget to 'see' the places we live. There are so many awesome things you can do that don't cost a cent.

Holidaying on the cheap

Everybody loves a holiday. It doesn't get much better than getting away from it all and taking in new sights, tastes, and experiences, or spending time with family and friends. But it doesn't have to cost a small fortune to do so.

- Do you love sleeping in, drinking by the pool, and having nice dinners? Ask yourself if you have to travel overseas to do this. You could save yourself thousands in airline tickets by staying in a cool hotel nearer to home instead of never leaving your resort in Fiji or Hawaii.

- Do you like getting a big group together? Check out Airbnb[32] or your local companies such as Bookabach[33] which offer some incredibly cheap deals by utilising someone else's holiday home. Large family groups can end up paying around $20 a head per night of accommodation. Cheapest family reunion ever!
- Do you love staying in 5-star hotels? Who doesn't! If you can book at the last minute you can get some awesome deals on sites like Lastminute[34], or if you're like me and that's not logistically possible, check out the mystery hotel deals some sites offer, or use Scoopon[35]

---

32 http://www.airbnb.com
33 http://www.bookabach.co.nz
34 http://www.lastminute.com.au
35 http://www.scoopon.com.au

or similar sites to get up to 80% off some fabulous places.

- Are you desperate for a sea change? Consider swapping houses with another family and saving yourself on accommodation costs. These can be close by or in totally different countries!

- If you just can't live without travelling overseas, try travelling in the off-peak season. Not only is it bucket loads cheaper, but there are fewer people, too! Or pick somewhere that none of your friends have been. Chances are, if it's off the beaten track, it will be cheaper and far more interesting!

- Pick countries that are cheap once you're there, like Thailand and Vietnam. While your flights will still be expensive, hotels and food are cheap.

- Get a job that has staff travel as a perk. I considered doing this for ages, and still think about it every time I pay full price for a fare. We have many friends who work for airlines, and while there are definitely downsides (like crazy hours and stupid people) heavily discounted travel is certainly a big draw card!

- Take advantage of companies like Ryanair[36] who do 1-penny fares to many destinations out of the UK. You can even book multiple fares in one go and have trips lined up all year. Then you only really have to pay for the airport taxes, accommodation, and food once on the ground.

- Find accommodation that has cooking facilities. See the countries you want, but save money by shopping at

---

36 http://www.ryanair.com

supermarkets and cooking your own food instead of eating out 3 times a day.

- Book airline tickets online rather than through a travel agent, and book flights on a Tuesday—Thursday as they are often cheaper then. If you can't do midweek flights, make sure you book well in advance when tickets are cheaper.

- Look at how much travel you will need to do in your holiday spot and if it will be cheaper to hire a rental car or to just use public transport or the occasional taxi.

  I recently did a trip to Tasmania with a couple of girlfriends, and we found it was cheaper to hire a car than to pay for transport and tours to take us to all the places we wanted to see.

- Stay outside the city. Sometimes it's heaps cheaper to stay in the town next door to where you want to explore—even with the cost of transport. Hotels know their little spot is a tourist Mecca and they charge accordingly.

- Speaking of tourist Mecca's, do you really need to visit them now? There are plenty of amazing spots in the world without visiting the same ones as everyone else. Leave them until you are mortgage free and can enjoy them in style!

- Check to see if the attractions you are visiting offer any age, occupation or student discounts. When we were travelling around Paris, my sister-in-law had a letter written in French stating she was a teacher, which got her discounted or free access to several attractions. We also got into quite a few places cheaper because we were under 21. Wouldn't work for me now! But it doesn't hurt to ask.

- Sign up for a travel-related credit card or use 'pointsbased' store cards. Here in Australia, Qantas points are a big plus for credit card companies. It takes a while to save up enough, but then you can get free flights anywhere on the Qantas network (with enough points), I mean free! You can't get much cheaper than that. Flybuys here in Australia also allow you to redeem your points for accommodation and car hire. If you buy a lot of groceries or use credit cards often, then these can be simple and cost effective holiday savers.

- Check out a package deal. Sometimes these are even cheaper than scouring through individual items yourself, with a fraction of the effort.

- Share the expense. Travel with friends or family and split the cost of accommodation, food, and transport. Not only is it cheaper, but you'll have some great company too.

- Travel your own backyard. This is my favourite. Coming from NZ, but living in Australia, I have had so many people say to me, "How lovely are the Marlborough Sounds/Franz Joseph Glacier/Mitre Peak?" And I blush and say, "Actually, I wouldn't know, I've never been."

How often do we look abroad for our holidays and neglect seeing some of the truly amazing things in our own backyard? Not only do you not have to pay for airfares, but you are working in your own dollar, you don't have to hire a car if you drive, and chances are you know the local sites where you can find cheap accommodation or a place to pitch your tent.

Since being in Australia, my family and I have seen many places that people living here their whole lives have never been. The same was true while we lived in the UK. We went everywhere! So don't forget about your own backyard. You never know what adventure awaits you. And next time someone asks you what a particular place is like, you can reply with confidence, "Yes, I've been there, and it was incredible!"

- Packing a picnic. The same reasoning applies if you and your family are going out for the day. In my house, we love the beach and we are there at least twice a week, all year round. Sometimes we stay for a few hours, other times we stay all day. I always pack food, water bottles, and in the winter, thermoses full of tea and hot chocolate. I can't even imagine how much we would have had to spend if we weren't as prepared. Don't even get me started on buying bottles of water. If you live in a First-World country, buy a reusable bottle and fill it yourself from the tap. Good for you, your pocket, and the environment!

- Going to the zoo, the movies, or a theme park? It's doubly important to pack your own food. Places like this that have a captive audience (nowhere else to shop) can charge whatever they want to for food and they invariably do, knowing people will be forced to pay for it or go hungry and thirsty. Personally, I'm stubborn and would just go hungry, but when you have kids that changes... A little bit of preparation can save you a lot of money in the long run.

Whatever you enjoy doing, keep doing it! There is nothing sadder than seeing someone give up everything they love for the wrong reasons. If you find you really can't afford any of the things you love, then revisit *Chapters 1-3* and re-think your budget and your spending. There should always be money for fun!

Key points:

- There are many ways to holiday without spending a fortune.

- Always allow money, and time, to continue doing the things you love.

- Do cheap activities often, the dearer ones occasionally, and save up for the expensive ones.

- Make sure you include some spending money in your budget.

- Life is for living. Live it!

Up next in *Chapter 12: Investing in Life,* we will talk about investment properties, goals, and planning ahead for the life you want to lead.

CHAPTER 12
INVESTING IN LIFE

"Screw it, let's do it!"—Richard Branson

Richard Branson, never one to mince words, has totally nailed my thoughts on investing. It has a bad rap because of market uncertainties, and frankly, because people jump into things without any knowledge whatsoever. And investing is a leap of faith. But if it were easy everyone would be doing it. Arm yourself with knowledge, seek advice from professionals, and take the leap.

Planning ahead

Look ahead and start planning what you want to do when you hand over your final payment. Travel? Invest in more property? Retire? While you might change your mind a few times between now and then, thinking about what you want now will start putting your options in front of you.

Don't drop the ball now, or you'll literally be kicking yourself as you watch your mortgage stretch out even longer.

Invest or nest?

If you're still living at home, are happy flatting with friends, are backpacking around the world, have a job that provides accommodation, or want to live in areas you can't afford to buy, you could look at buying a home for investment purposes rather than living in it yourself.

When you buy a home for you, there are things that you ask yourself that you just don't need to with an investment property.

- Would I want to live here for a long time?

- Is it close enough to work?

- Are there things I enjoy doing in the vicinity?

- Does the house have a pool/big yard/spare room?

These and many other things are important to you, but not necessarily to other people.

When you buy an investment property, the 'things to look for' list still rings true. Generally, the local area and cost-based assessments you do when buying a home for yourself are also true when renting it to others. Nobody wants to live in a crumbling dive, in a gang—and crime-ridden area.

Some other things to ask yourself though, may include:

- What is the rental yield?

- Is the property close to universities, hospitals, business districts, or areas that people want to bring up children in? Is it in a place that will get permanent rent?

- Or is it close to ski fields, beaches, lakes, national parks, etc., that people want to visit seasonally, and will you get plenty of holiday rentals at higher prices?

- How much will your outgoings be each month?

- Does it need much work done to it to gain maximum returns? You can't buy a wreck and do it up while living in it if it's an investment property. It has to be immediately liveable or you have to be willing to spend some money on it to make it that way.

What is rental yield?

Rental yield is the amount of money you get from your property after paying your outgoings.

It can be worked out two different ways—gross or net. To get the gross return you calculate the yearly rent and divide it by the cost of the property, then times it by 100.

For example: The $500,000 sample house rents for $600 a week or $31,200 a year. $31,200 divided by $500,000 is 0.0624. Times this by 100 and you have a rental yield of 6.2%. If the property, however, only cost you $300,000 and you were still getting $600 a week in rent, then you would have a cracking yield of 10.4%.

MORTGAGE AMOUNT	YEARLY RENT	RENT DIVIDED BY MORTGAGE X 100	TOTAL RENTAL YIELD
$150,000	$31,200	$31,200 ÷ $150,000 x 100	20.8%
$300,000	$31,200	$31,200 ÷ $300,000 x 100	10.4%
$500,000	$31,200	$31,200 ÷ $500,000 x 100	6.2%
$750,000	$31,200	$31,200 ÷ $750,000 x 100	4.1%
$1,000,000	$31,200	$31,200 ÷ $1,000,000 x 100	3.1%

Calculating the gross yield is definitely the easiest, but the net yield is much more accurate. It requires you to enter a lot more variables, known or estimated, to give you a better picture of property costs. Houses with a high gross yield may end up having a worse net yield than a similar property, if there are more expenses involved.

These can include building and pest inspections, legal expenses, and ongoing costs like insurances, repairs, and maintenance, and management fees. As you can see in our example, working out the net value on our two properties gives you actual yields of 7.2% and 4.3%, considerably lower than the gross yield.

PROPERY EXPENSES	$300,000 LOAN	$500,000 LOAN
Rental Income	$31,200	$31,200
Bank Fees	$120	$240
Accountant fees	$300	$210
Maintenance and Repairs	$965	$715
Advertising	$180	$35
Property management	$4,650	$4,200
Insurance	$1,500	$1,700
Council rates	$1,700	$2,500
Total	$9,415	$9,600
Net rental yield	7.2%	4.3%

Building a property portfolio

Is it better to buy several cheap properties, or one dearer one?

Often there is a reason there are vast price differences in properties within the same area, and they aren't usually good ones! That said, if you are looking at houses in several different areas, then look to the yields. Ask the real estate agent for rental appraisals and work out gross rental yields.

Using equity to buy many homes with good financial yields can be a great way to earn a lot of money fast. People always seem to see the benefits, however, and none of the negatives.

There are a lot of costs and risks involved in buying multiple properties, and you need to take all of them into account. Do your homework and do your figures. Don't just look at the rental return!

Buying multiple properties off the previous home's equity is like an elephant balancing on a ball. It's a great show while it lasts, but one little slip can lead to catastrophe. When all of your homes are mortgaged, and you don't have a freehold property to fall back on, you could end up selling homes at a loss just to cover the other mortgages. This could be because of interest rate rises, downturns in the housing market, rental yields dropping, or any one of hundreds of other reasons.

A safer alternative to simultaneously buying properties is this: Just buy one. Pour everything you have into paying off the mortgage as fast as you can, and once it's gone, buy another one.

Doing this will give you a solid foundation to build on, and a mortgage free home to buffer you against any problems you may encounter in the future.

Then, combine the rent from your first house and add it to the rent from a second property, and watch the mortgage rapidly decline. Once that's paid off, you buy a third. See where I'm going with this? This method is akin to a skyscraper. Each story is built faster than the last one and you can build it as high as you like. There are no limits, and because each floor is built on the solid level below it, if something untoward happens, only one floor will be lost.

Many people have made fortunes by buying a property, using its equity to buy another, and so on, till they have 18 homes or more. Many people have also lost fortunes. At least if you are paying off mortgages before purchasing your next property, the dangers are not so inherent. Yes, it will probably be a slower financial curve, but a much safer one.

Using your equity to invest

Our friend Leo told us that when our mortgage reached $100,000 we should buy another house as an investment property.

The thought of having more than one mortgage terrified me— all that debt! But I couldn't ignore the obvious benefits of doing just that, and when my husband got a new job it pushed us to truly consider it as a tax break. You don't need to have your house totally paid off to buy another one. You can use the equity from your existing home to finance it. What is equity? Essentially, your home's worth, minus the debt. So, if you have a home that is now worth $700,000 and you only owe $150,000, you would have $550,000 in equity. You find a house that has a good rental return for $200,000, and the bank gives you a second mortgage.

You don't have to pay anything out of your own pocket and the bank doesn't care, because if something bad happens they have a home that is worth far more that they can take. Did you hear what I said? If you stuff up your investment and you need to sell up, or can't make your payments, the bank will selvage all the costs it can, but ultimately, your first home is riding on the line. The bank will take it and sell it, even at a loss, to regain their money, so be careful!

That said, equity is a fantastic thing. It saves you going through all the mortgage hoopla again, and you don't have to try and save money when you should be paying off your mortgage. If you do decide to buy an investment property, set the mortgage to interest only and use all your earnings to pay off your home loan sooner.

Do you want to use your equity? Knowing what your property is worth is vital. Watch the market. Keep an eye on your local property mag and see what is happening to properties similar to yours. Are they going up? Dropping? Holding? Keeping your finger on the property pulse can give you valuable insight into what you should do, when.

Whether this would benefit you is something you would have to talk to your accountant about. Don't go off half-cocked thinking you're going to buy 21 properties and live off the rent like lady muck. While that can work, you have to know what you're doing. A lot of the research we covered when buying your first home or investment property is the same for buying subsequent ones, but there are other tricks you can use too.

You can purchase a home to use as a holiday house. Sometimes homes are only seasonally viable, but the money you make, say over a snow season, is more than enough to cover mortgage repayments; you can then use it as a holiday base for the rest of the year without paying a red cent. Make sure if you buy elsewhere that you don't have to pay taxes for income earned in both the country of residence and the country of purchase.

This is a trap for young players and can turn a financially viable property into a money pit.

Our accountant once said that while he had invested in pretty much everything at some time or other, property was the only thing he had never lost money on. It is generally a much safer investment than other things. If your property takes a downward shift, as long as you are prepared to sit on it, you can almost guarantee it will eventually rise back up again.

There are no tax breaks for a mortgage on your own home in Australia, only for investment properties. So focus on your own mortgage first, and once that's gone, then you can focus on paying off your investment. In America it may be better to pay off investment properties first, as there *are* tax breaks on personal mortgages.

Whichever way the cookie crumbles, you will end up with a true passive income stream with only minimal expenses to cover. It's everyone's dream, isn't it?

Tax concessions

Who earns the most? Our first investment property will hopefully be a holiday home. Because this won't make a great deal of money, it will go under my husband's name, to decrease his taxable income. However, our accountant told us if we found a really high-yield investment, then that should go in my name, as I only work part time, so the extra income wouldn't bump my tax into a higher bracket.

Make sure if you are putting things in one person's name that you protect yourself legally. What happens to that house if you separate and it is only in one person's name? Speak to a lawyer and suss out your options. Don't go into anything half-arsed. It never ends well.

Negative gearing

In Australia we have something called negative gearing. It is also legal in New Zealand and Canada, but is illegal in every other country. Essentially, it allows you to take the losses made from a rental property or other investment, such as mortgage interest, insurances and maintenance, and use them to lower your taxable income rate.

For example: Paul earns $80,000 a year. His investment property makes him $10,000 in rent but costs him $23,000 in interest and expenses over the year. So, his taxable income, instead of being $90,000 (income + rent) becomes $67,000. He saves $7,925 in tax. This means he has only really made a loss of around $15,000.

	NON GEARED INCOME	NEGATIVE GEARED INCOME
Wages	$80,000	$80,000
Rental income	$10,000	$10,000
Rental expenses	-$23,000	-$23,000
Tax payable	$21,247	$13,322
Net income	$45,753	$53,678

If you are paying higher taxes and your rental losses drop you into a lower tax bracket, then you may find you are actually better off financially from a tax perspective too. It is very easy to work out how much tax you will pay or save using online tax tools. This one was made using our local government's tax calculator.

While there is no negative gearing in the United States, there are tax breaks for your mortgage interest payments. If you are looking at investing, not just paying off your mortgage, it could be better to pay off your investment properties before your own mortgage. This is something you would need to discuss with your accountant.

There are plenty of people who know more about negative gearing than me, as well as online calculators, but the point I'm trying to make is this: An investment property is not black and white. There are many little things that can make a huge difference to your back pocket, which you need to nut out before committing yourself. Do your research and speak with professionals, such as your accountant or a property investor, before jumping in.

Why you shouldn't put all your eggs in one basket

Protect your money. Don't put all your eggs in one basket. If you like working the stock market, great, but put some money in property, or buy gold and silver as well. At least then, if everything goes to pot, you shouldn't lose everything.

I look at what is happening financially around the world and I get worried. Banks are not giving out money. Stock markets are losing trillions overnight. It's scary stuff. Look at putting your properties and investments into a family trust. If something does happen and you are declared bankrupt, or you drop dead, at least the government cannot touch it if it's not in your name. It also gives you the ability to choose who ends up with the dividends of your hard work.

Diversify, and keep your fingers in lots of pies!

Goals and how to achieve them

If you are not setting goals and striving to reach them every day, then you will never be able to dictate your direction in life.

There is something to be said for taking each day as it comes and allowing happenstance to steer you in new directions, but if you are trying to get ahead and you want something specific in life, then *be* specific.

Know what you want. Write it down and then work towards making it a reality.

"No-one knows what he can do until he tries."—Pubilius Syrus

So try. If you don't reach your goals, try again or try something new. You will never meet a goal you do not set, that's for damn sure!

Look at Richard Branson's Top 10 Tips for Making Lists[37] and begin doing it today! He pretty much nails it.

Set easy-to-reach goals, and set goals so far out Neil Armstrong would have trouble reaching them.

Don't be discouraged if you don't reach them all; be inspired by what you have achieved.

Wake up every morning and remind yourself what you're working for. Even a man who takes one step a day will eventually reach his goal.

If you're still sitting around the campfire talking about starting, you will never arrive.

---

[37] http://www.virgin.com/richard-branson/top-10-tips-formaking-lists

Don't let your doubts get in the way of amazing things.

Wow, I think I missed my calling in life. I should have written inspirational cards...

Seriously, though, if you want to live life to the max, have a passive income, and do the things you enjoy with the people you love, then plan on making that happen.

Hell, if you want to be an ant farmer or a professional fly fisherman, then make a plan and set it in motion.

No one is going to do it for you. Plan to succeed.

Creating a passive income stream

My goal has always been to retire by 40. Not just me, but my husband too. I want to travel, play an instrument, write, eat, learn another language, and live life to its fullest.

While I won't quite hit my target, I don't think I'll be far off. I am working on creating a passive income source for us that will pay for all our adventures, while only doing the absolute minimum. For me, this means writing books and investing in real estate.

For you it might mean creating a property portfolio, inventing something awesome, or creating a website that builds revenue. I don't know what you're good at, but you do! Don't make paying off your house the final step; make it the first. Not only will you be a step ahead of the curve, you'll be living the life you always wanted.

Don't quit your job just yet, though. You might be about to pay off your mortgage, but you still need to live, right? Unless you are actually at retirement age and have enough super or savings to carry you through, in which case retire and enjoy it mortgage free!

Work smarter, not harder

While putting in an extra shift several times a week might seem like a great idea to boost the bank account, you can't keep doing it forever. Eventually your body and your mind get tired, you're more prone to sickness and mistakes, and all the effort you put into scraping those extra dollars together goes down the drain.

Not paying double mortgage payments will leave you with a huge chunk of free money. Take courses to up-skill yourself, be the go-to person in your industry if it's something you enjoy. If you're happy in your job, then take more time for yourself. Go on a long weekend even if it means taking unpaid leave. Live. And enjoy living.

Is there something different you always wanted to try? A business venture or a new career path? Now is the time. You no longer have the excuse of time or money to hold you back. Follow your heart and be one of the few people who enjoy their jobs!

You have carved out a stack of breathing room for yourself. You no longer have to spend all your earnings on a mortgage. You just have to make enough to cover the bills and keep yourself in the manner in which you've become accustomed, so not much! And you should be sweet.

Instead of clocking up more hours, use some of our tips to make money while you're at work, or to create a passive income. The aim of this book is not to turn you into a workaholic who watches life pass on by, it is to arm you with tools that help you work smarter, make use of what you have, and funnel those gains into creating an unstoppable future.

Key points:

- Plan ahead and decide what you want to do in the future.

- Creative a passive income for yourself and work smarter—not harder.

- Don't put all your eggs into one basket when investing.

- Take advantage of tax breaks and concessions.

- Use your equity to invest in real estate and build a property portfolio.

- If using your property as an investment, look for things others will find appealing and check the net rental yield before purchasing.

Almost at the end of the line, peeps. Conclusion, up next.

CONCLUSION

"Every ending is a new beginning"—Marianne Williamson

The last dance—your final payment

You just handed over your final payment. Your mortgage account now reads $0.00 owing and you and your bank have parted ways. Well, if you haven't already bought another property, that is!

What an amazing feeling. You feel like you're going to explode, you're so happy!!

You can't help it. You find yourself babbling excitedly to your friends and family even though you feel a bit crap that they are still slogging away with theirs. But yours is done! Woo-hoo!

Letting your crazy loose

Give yourself time to go crazy, to spend that money you never had to spend. Buy a whole new wardrobe of clothes. Go on a holiday or two. Or three! Buy a better car, a new surfboard, or a flash new TV. Whatever floats your boat, really. A boat! There's an idea...

Celebrate with friends and give yourself the kudos you deserve. You put in the hard yards and it really paid off. Learn how to spend money on little things again. Buy a coffee. Shout your mates to lunch, or a round. Goodness knows they probably deserve it after putting up with you and your antics for the past 10 years!

Taking stock—and your next step

When you've calmed down a bit, take stock. Review what you've learnt over the past ten years, how you've grown as a person, and what changes you like and what you don't. Give yourself a new goal. It might not be buying another property, it could be finishing the house, writing a book, or learning a language.

Whatever you decide to do with the rest of your life, take the lessons you've learnt and apply them. You are now stronger, in a better financial situation, and know yourself better than many people ever will.

Even if you use only a fraction of the knowledge in this book, you will be ahead of the game and have more financial freedom to do what you love every day, instead of one day.

If you have the desire and the knowledge to change, don't let doubts hold you back.

"Stretch yourself. You might just like what's possible"—Jamie Gerdsen

Be proud of yourself. I know I am

BONUS MATERIAL

Want more? Head to www.how2without.com for free access to bonus materials such as printable checklists and worksheets that will help you achieve your goal of financial freedom.

Worksheets

- Budgeting

- Cutting the Fat

- Making More Moola

- Debt—and how to get rid of it

- The Magic Formula

- Home Costs

- Then and Now

- Life's a Ride

- Looking Forward

Checklists

- Good Bank—Great Mortgage

- High Risk

- Picking a great area

- My Home

- Open Homes

- Renovation

LINKS FROM BOOK

In order of appearance:

www.How2Without.com—Free downloadable worksheets and checklists for this book and all our other books. www.goget.com.au—Local car hire by the half hour.

www.carnextdoor.com.au—Neighbour to neighbour car sharing.

www.wordpress.com—Create a personal blog or business site.

www.kitchensurfing.com—Matches you with chefs that cook meals for you in your own home.

www.shutterstock.com—Subscriptions and images on demand for every budget.

www.istockphoto.com—Royalty-free images, illustrations, videos, and music clips at great prices.

www.etsy.com—Online market for craft supplies and handmade goods.

https://xe172.isrefer.com/go/curcust/HeidiF. (Please note this is an affiliate link for Self Publishing School). Online course that teaches you how to write and publish a bestselling book. This fantastic course got me where I am today. I love writing, but had no idea how to go about publishing my book. Self-publishing school provided the knowledge and support I needed to get my book published, and to turn it into a bestseller!

http://www.quitn6.ontraport.com/t?orid=8475&opid=
1 (Please note this is an affiliate link for Quitn6). Book
series on how to quit the job you hate and do what you
love in 6 months. This FREE series inspired me to get
this book out there for all you lovely readers, and to do
what I love every day—not one day!

www.udemy.com—Online site with thousands of
courses.

www.freecarmedia.com/—Use your car as a mobile
billboard.

www.advercar.com/—Use your car as a mobile
billboard.

www.airbnb.com—Rent your home to make income.

www.macrobusiness.com.au—Snapshot of
Demographia's affordability survey.

www.ahuri.edu.au—Affordability and access to home
ownership.

www.demographia.com/dhi.pdf—Housing
Affordability Over 9 Nations Study.

www.thesimpledollar.com—Debt today in comparison
to the 1970's.

www.demandinstitute.org—Article on baby boomers
and their homes. www.couchsurfing.com—Stay with
locals for free. www.domain.com.au—Strata levies.

www.domain.com.au—Price estimates for properties
in Australia. www.styleathome.com—Return on
renovation costs. www.bookabach.co.nz—Holiday
rental accommodation around NZ.

www.lastminute.com.au—Last minute deals on hotels, flights, and experiences Australia-wide.

http://www.scoopon.com.au—Heavily discounted deals around Australia.

www.ryanair.com—Economy airline flying out of the UK.

www.virgin.com/richard-branson/top-10-tips-formaking-lists—Richard Branson's top 10 tips for making lists.

DICTIONARY
EXPRESSIONS AND TERMS

A bucket load—*A large amount, or number*

A decent whack—*A fair amount*

Ad hoc—*Improvised, thrown together, casual basis*

A dump—*An unpleasant or dreary place*

Bespoke—*Made to order for a specific person or purpose*

Bucks—*money or dollars*

Burns a hole in your pocket—*Money that you have just acquired but are eager to spend*

Chugging along—*Doing what needs to be done at a weary pace*

Clocking up—*To accumulate, reach large numbers*

Co-contributions—*Where more than one party contributes or takes part in something*

Conniption—*A fit of rage or hysterics*

Crappy/crap—*horrible, cheap, awful, bad*

Credit rating—*An estimate of a persons' ability to fulfil their financial requirements*

Dead money—*A monetary investment that is likely to fail or has no real value*

Debt consolidation—*Taking out one large loan to pay off many smaller ones*

Direct debit—*An automatic transfer from your bank to a third party on a regular basis*

Elephant in the room—*An obvious truth that is being ignored or going unaddressed*

Goes to pot—*Deteriorate, decline, go to ruin*

Grand—*Slang for one thousand dollars*

Granny flat—*Self-contained accommodation suitable for an elderly relative*

Grey water system—*Domestic wastewater that is re-used for things like gardening*

Gross—*An amount of money without tax or other contributions having been deducted*

Incidentals—*Extras, contingencies, odds and ends, expenses*

Kick arse—*Really cool, great, fantastic, amazing*

Knock off (debt)—*Get rid of, finish*

Kryptonite—*A person's weakness, or something that makes them weak*

Lucrative—*Producing a great deal of profit*

Median Multiple (houses)—*Ratio between median house price and median household income*

Moola—*money*

No brainer—*Something that requires little or no mental effort*
Periodically—*Something that reoccurs after intervals of time*

Perk—*A special privilege or side benefit*

Plug it in/into—*Put it in, type it in*

Propensity—*An inclination or natural tendency*

Reno—*Shortened version of renovation*

Repertoire—*Collection, stock, range*

Retail therapy—*The practice of shopping to make yourself happier*

Roaring trade—*Lively or successful, thriving*

Sea change—*A profound or notable transformation or change*

Schmuck—*A foolish or contemptible person*

Scrounge—*Borrow or obtain something, usually through stealth or the generosity of others*

Shelling out—*Pay or give out money for something, usually unwillingly*

Shuttle (people)—*Move, drive around, travel back and forth*

Skyrocket—*A price, rate, or amount increasing very steeply or rapidly*

Smackaroos—*Slang for money*

Spewing—*Very upset, mad, angry*

Staying under 5 stars—*Staying in a 5-star hotel*

Sucks—*Not good, bad, expression of sympathy* Sweet—*Awesome, fantastic, great*

Tax bracket—*A range of incomes taxed at a particular rate*

Tourist Mecca—*An attraction that many people visit, usually famous for something*

Under the axe—*Something to be cut or chopped*

Vetting/vet—Appraisal, background check on a person

WTF—*Why the face. Why, what were you thinking?*

Your own backyard—*The area near where you live*

ACKNOWLEDGEMENTS

Special thanks to my wonderful family, who bought me up knowing the value of a dollar, and the pros and cons of having (and not having) money. Thank you, Mum, for teaching me how to budget, and Clinton for teaching me how to stick to it! To my beautiful daughter who makes all my hard work worthwhile with her gorgeous smile and unending cheekiness.

To my amazing family; I am so grateful for your constant support and for helping me with every step of my life and every portion of this book.

Massive thanks especially go to my Mum, brother, and two sisters, who provided technical help and incredible amounts of feedback and editing of my book, and to my lovely editor Elaine who took out all the kinks. Thank you all for your help and encouragement. Thank you Laura for stepping up and designing my cover when nothing was working. I love it!

Thank you Matt Stone for your Quitn6 books. They inspired me, encouraged me, and gave me the 'gee-up' I needed to get going! And they were FREE! I don't care what they say about you. You're all right. (-:

To all the wonderful people at SPS—you guys rock! I could always count on you for knowledge, encouragement and support.

And finally to all my friends, family, and fans, who provided feedback and reviews and made my book what it is today— thank you, from the bottom of my heart.

ABOUT THE AUTHOR

Heidi lives in sunny Sydney with her husband, daughter, and dog Gonzo, where she likes to swim, rock climb, and sew. She grew up in beautiful New Zealand, famous for 'kiwi ingenuity'—and of course rugby!—and also spent 2-1/2 years living in and wandering around England and Europe. She has been writing for many years, although this is her first nonfiction book.

She loves hanging out with family, travelling, tasting new foods, and exploring everything life has to offer.

Mortgage Free is the first of what will be many books in her How2Without series.